# UNDEFINED NATURALLY
## CRAFTING A FLORAL ART PRACTICE
### AN ARTIST'S MEMOIR ON DESIGN AND PROCESS

JUAN M. VILLANUEVA

Disclaimer: This is a work of original authorship. While it includes personal stories, observations, and reflections, it is intended for informational and inspirational purposes only. Any resemblance to actual persons, living or dead, is purely coincidental unless expressly stated. The content of this book may reference topics related to mental health, physical well-being, business practices, and financial decision-making. These references are based solely on the author's personal experience and are not intended to constitute or substitute for professional medical, mental health, financial, or legal advice. The author makes no representations or warranties concerning the accuracy, applicability, or completeness of the content. Readers are strongly encouraged to seek guidance from appropriately licensed professionals before making decisions or changes related to their health, finances, or business activities.

The author and publisher disclaim any liability, loss, or risk incurred as a consequence, directly or indirectly, of the use or application of any content in this publication.

Cover design by Juan M. Villanueva
Published by Floral and Gardens Press ©
www.floralandgardens.com
ISBN: 979-8-9997474-1-9
First Edition

For Mom.

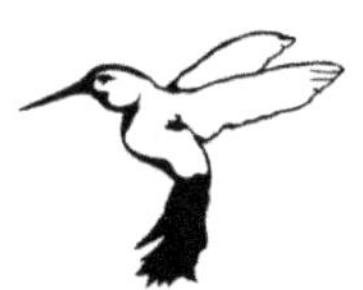

CONTENTS


**INTRODUCTION**   01

## PART I: FOUNDATION

01 GETTING STARTED   07

02 CREATING SPACE   21

03 THE SKILLS   35

04 WHY   47

05 THE CREATIVE PROCESS   55

## PART II: FORMATION

06 PATIENCE   77

07 ON LEADERSHIP   91

08 FAILURE   107

09 INTENTION   119

10 FEAR   129

## PART III: PERSPECTIVE

11 RESPECT   145

12 BUILDING MOMENTUM   157

13 DEFINING SUCCESS   169

## PART IV: METHOD

14 EVENT PRIMER   187

# INTRODUCTION

Dusk is setting in. A glazed stare out the window.

Fireflies flutter in the hazy, sweltering summer air. Cicadas buzz in lockstep in the large live oak that grows, regal and commanding, outside the kitchen window. That tree and the woman who commands the space within were always like one and the same to me.

Lying on my belly, nibbling clover, I watch a black tarantula scurry across the bed of my *Abuela's* rose garden.

"Will we be the last generation to see fireflies?" I wonder, recalling what I'd recently read, as I pull the shades.

It's raining again as I write this. A grey, ominous sky drapes the high-rises across midtown Manhattan in clouds and fog. It's cooler than usual for mid-June, and it's another signal that the world is shifting, both within and without.

It's been a long journey from those sticky summer evenings in South Texas to here: the city, the work, the words. Like many of us, I've been adjusting to what once passed as normal. Even routines bend differently now. Expectations shift more sharply and abruptly. The form it now takes may change, but the thread remains the same.

Over time, my practice has moved across disciplines: from event florals to bio-art installations, from welding to photography, from muddy garden beds to classrooms and stages. But at my core, I'm simply an artist. This statement is not something I claim lightly. That title was not a given. It's something I've had to earn in the course of a never-ending search for new ways to share my story and to explore the truth.

To be honest, this isn't the artist's life I once imagined. Sustaining a creative practice has turned out to be more layered, unpredictable, and, at times, unorthodox than I ever expected. While the bulk of my work and income revolves around floral design, my artistic identity is imbued in everything I do. The lines between art, commerce, and survival are often blurred, and this book lives in that intersection.

In many ways, the work has always been my catalyst for change. In this latest project, I've begun teaching myself how to resee my story. Because I'm still learning how to receive my flowers. Many florists are.

**Why I Wrote This Book:**

I don't claim to be a writer by trade, but this book was called to be made. It was sparked by students' voices and long-held questions that demanded answers. And from a deep sense of knowing that said, "Now is the time." What you hold is the result of that pull: imperfect, honest, and raw.

This book began as a way to make sense of what the work had become. Through writing, it became a way to map and articulate what I've learned over the years. This work, this book, has been anything but a straightforward process. It came together slowly, stitching memories and lessons word by word, while reexamining the stories I clung to about them. If something here resonates, then I trust it's found the reader it was meant for. That's all I ever hoped for, not perfection, but connection.

What's emerged here is a hybrid of sorts: part memoir, part creative philosophy, part instructional guide. Not quite a self-help, not quite a how-to. I see it as a work, filled with signposts pointing a way for anyone navigating the complex, bewildering, and often circuitous path of making a life in art.

**How to Use This Work:**

The following pages offer what I've learned about respecting the process and following through to its conclusion. The stories included are deeply personal, shaped by my lived experience. In them, I offer guidance, but I don't dictate a path. It's more of a conversation, mirroring the kinds of discussions I've had with students, peers, and mentors over the years.

If you're here for the nuts and bolts of floral event instruction, feel free to skip ahead to Part 4. That section includes a sixteen-point primer that walks through the full arc of a floral event, from concept to execution. But if I may suggest, the rest of the book may resonate more than you expect. And if floristry isn't your focus, that part can be skipped entirely.

Throughout, I've done my best not to tell you what to do. As I often remind my students, "I can't teach you anything. The best I can do is show you what's worked for me." The real learning happens in the doing, with your own hands, in your own time, and in your own practice.

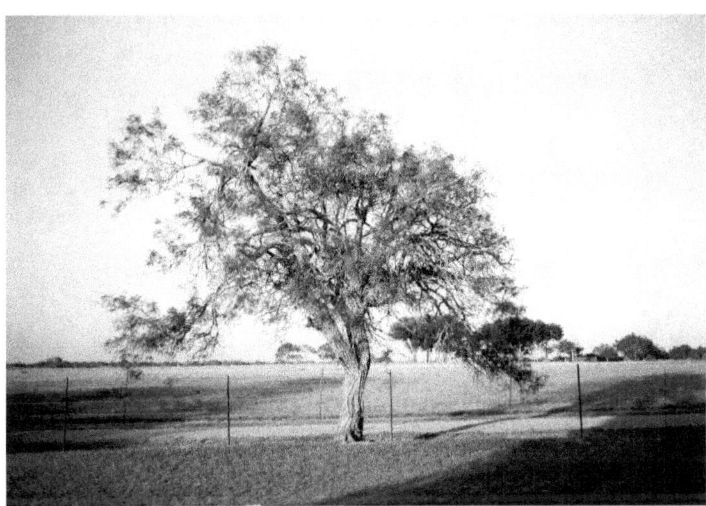

The mesquite tree on the family ranch symbolizes the resilience of the land, worked by generations. Photo by me.

# PART I:

## FOUNDATION

Laying the physical, mental, and creative groundwork for a sustainable practice to take root.

# 1

## GETTING STARTED

I grew up in South Texas, on my grandfather's cattle ranch just outside a small town called Alice. My hometown has been slowly declining in population since its heyday in the late 1980s and early 1990s. My family came from calloused hands and long days: ranchers, bar owners, school cooks, and carpenters. Our roots in that land run deep, and go back to when the land was still Mexico, maybe even more ancient still. But we were never the kind of people who kept records. Just stories. And scars.

I was the middle child, the only boy. Growing up on the ranch with my two sisters was a bit isolating. Our closest neighbor's ranch was around a quarter mile from our home. This meant I had to create my own entertainment and company. I loved it. My playground was *El Monte*, The Woods, on that fifty-acre plot of land, where we had our trailer house. The Mesquite trees were my jungle gym. The Prickly Pears were target practice for my slingshot and pellet gun. We were always surrounded by a variety of animals, including cows, ducks, turkeys, chickens, and peacocks. Basically, all the domesticated ones, at one point or another. They would become my companions and sworn enemies. It was wild and alive. When we lost the lease on our trailer, we had to move out and into town. It felt as if we had been torn from something vital. That soil, that land, was always home and still is.

My parents separated soon after. And eventually, after hopping around South Texas for a few years, my mother opened a flower shop back in our hometown, not because she had the time or the money, but because she had the nerve. Before that, she'd spent years working odd jobs, cashiering at grocery stores, and at fast food spots. Starting a business was undoubtedly a risk. But I think she needed to build something for herself after our family came apart.

During this time, I ended up living with my grandmother in a small house that everyone referred to as hers, even though my grandfather was alive and under the same roof. That house became a kind of harbor for me. Even though it was chaotic at times, family stopped in to catch a home-cooked lunch, or dropped off the *niños* to babysit. But it was stable in a way I had been craving for quite some time.

I drew constantly. Art was my oxygen. At one point, I planned to apply to the Air Force Academy, but that dream fell away when my grandmother had a massive stroke. Don't let this bum you out. She recently celebrated her 99th birthday, but at the time, life tilted on its axis. That was one of the first of several sharp turns to come.

I ended up in Chicago at the School of the Art Institute, full of raw talent and no plan. There, I took the required first-year foundational classes, focusing on sculpture and painting, but spent too much time chasing fantasies of the artist lifestyle and pot smoke. Even so, I was praised and encouraged to apply for a scholarship in sculpture, but I let it all slide. Missed deadlines. Lost funding. I thought the world would bend toward my 'genius.' It didn't. So, with no other options, I dropped out, ashamed and unbound.

What followed were years of improvisation: folding shirts in dusty stockrooms, teaching in community centers, drifting along. I lived on borrowed futons and an old student ID, sneaking back into painting studios because I didn't know where else to go. At one of my lowest points, wandering aimlessly around Chicago, a friend from South Texas found me rummaging through a thrift store, looked me dead in the eye, and said, "I know you had to drop out of school because you couldn't afford it, but you've got to do something. Anything. Learn a trade, air conditioners, cars, flowers, whatever. But you gotta do something with your life."

So I did, reluctantly. I walked into a flower shop and asked for a job, promising myself that it would only be until the art took off. To my surprise, it was the first thing that gave me structure without asking me to pretend. I started as a shop boy, then a small arrangement maker, and eventually, someone they could trust. I began to learn the pulse of the work; the quiet urgency of perishable beauty. Flowers don't wait. They teach you about timing and attention, about surrendering control. They rot if you ignore them. They reward continued, consistent care. And, teach you nonattachment in scores.

I didn't realize it at the time, but that was the beginning of a new kind of discipline. One that was seasonal, imperfect, and rooted in process more than product. I already had the grand vision, but what I really needed was to ease into the flow

In rooting into that rhythm, I came to realize that time is the most valuable resource we possess. This book begins from there, with recognizing and implementing the patterns that made the dream possible.

**The Myth of the Muse:**

In this initial chapter, we focus on getting started rather than striving for brilliance. We lay a groundwork, prioritizing movement over rupture and presence over perfection. Let's start there.

Inspiration isn't something I wait around for. It's not magic, or mood, or even *ganas*, desire, most days. It's rhythm. Early on, I bought into the myth that artists are meant to drift, waiting for some divine flash, chasing chaos because it's somehow more real. But that never worked for me. Not for long. What saved me, what actually kept me creating, wasn't waiting for the muse, no, no, no. It was showing up, at the same time, in the same place, again and again, on schedule. Not always knowing what would come of it.

As I see it, finding the muse has little to do with trapping lightning in a bottle, and more to do with tending the all too often low smoldering fire. And yeah, sometimes that means making stuff that doesn't work, because honestly, some days that damn light just goes out. But even the off days are part of the process. I've come to trust that.

**Create a Schedule:**

To begin, I can not overstress how much having a schedule and sticking to it has transformed my life. This, regrettably, is something I didn't truly set into practice until later in my life. A schedule sets the order of my day and creates small goals that carry me throughout the creative process. Without a schedule, it's as if I'm running around in the dark, fluttering in the wind, with no actual direction. Having a structured schedule makes me accountable. I know that kind of structure can be frightening, especially when you've grown up thinking freedom means doing whatever you want. This was me in my college days. But structure doesn't have to be confinement.

A schedule gives you tangible metrics. It shows you whether you're moving toward your goals or just in circles. Small victories inside a day can become massive turning points across a life.

Having a schedule is the backbone of doing the work: showing up every day, taking one step, no matter how small, toward the dream.

And, no, I'm not dictating what that needs to be in your life. This has to be your schedule. No one else can design it for you. Only you know how you work best. The point is to have a plan, get your affairs in order, and begin.

**My Schedule:**

My schedule varies because my work is deeply seasonal. What follows is a pared-down version of a day in the life, recognizing that there is no typical one, as each shifts with the season, the weather, or the work.

One consistency is my morning routine. I don't always wake at five, as part of some type of wake-up and grind club. I do, however, carve out two to three quiet hours before the studio. This allows me the time to get my mind in a positive space before getting into my day. I start with coffee, let's be honest, usually more than one cup, and a quiet video playing in the background. Affirmations, or tonal sound healing, act as small counterweights to the internal noise. During this time, if I am not quietly meditating on this, I typically create a morning automatic sketch or do some journaling, which also helps get this new programming downloaded into my subconscious.

> ***Quick Tip:*** *To help with time blindness, I often use video length as a soft timer. Replaying familiar ones so I can track time without needing to check the clock.*

I then eat, hydrate, and go through the rest of my morning routine of getting ready. As I finish my final cup of coffee, I allow myself to check emails or post on social media before heading out. This is not always perfect, but it is a small starting point by which I can begin to gauge success.

Generally speaking, I'll either be off to the studio to paint all day (my wife calls it "At the studio today"), or prepping for a floral event, sending flowers to a client's home, or gardening. This is pretty consistent. Floral days mean an early call time, typically 7-8 am. For private clients and garden work, I usually can't get into their homes till after 10 a.m. So I can arrive at the studio a bit later. Finally, for the at-studio days, I get there at my leisure, but typically no later than 10 am.

On floral days, I usually finish by mid-afternoon, often wrapping at clients' homes before the rhythms of family life return. On these shorter days, I may return to the studio to paint for a couple of hours, especially if I'm deeply involved with a piece. If I don't stay to paint, I will go home, usually to eat, and get going again on paperwork, working on QuickBooks for accounting till around 7 or 8. Finally, I leave the rest of my evening as free time to watch TV with my wife, gaming, or researching upcoming projects.

**Seasonal Adjustments:**

Depending on the season, there are some variations that serve as industry hallmarks.

### <u>Winter (December-March)</u>

The holidays see the big squeeze as we press every minute out of the available daylight. The work can include decorating for the holidays, getting flowers sent out for holiday parties, and getting our gifts out before the City shuts down around the 22nd of December. After that, it gets quiet...I mean dead quiet. Luckily, we receive a significant Javits Center event in mid-to-late February, which helps fiscally. Likewise, many florists will pick up again for the weeks around Valentine's Day. After Valentine's Day, we rest till spring officially begins. This is my time to dive into any art projects I may have neglected.

> *Side Bar: Almost all florists HATE Valentine's Day, a dirty little secret in the industry. The holiday is overwhelming, and prices soar due to demand. And the pressure on fulfilling last-minute services has increased significantly over the years. That said, brick-and-mortar shops can earn up to a quarter of their annual profits in just one week alone.*

### <u>Spring (April-June)</u>

As a gardener in New York City, spring seems to start with the first 70-degree day we get. This begins the two-month calming and negating of clients' panic and fears that they're missing the planting window for spring and summer. In May, though, projects truly start ramping up, and it is all hands on deck to fill all the orders and plantings we can handle before people head out to their summer homes, typically in the Hamptons.

### Summer (July-September)

There's a noticeable lull in the summer, punctuated by occasional events, as we settle into a regular routine of garden maintenance. While this period may become somewhat monotonous, it can also be quite enjoyable. I have started taking career development classes in the summer, leaving time to make art if I'm not taking a class or enjoying a client's garden in their absence. Then, around the second week of September, people trickle back into the city, and once all the Jewish holidays pass, the pace picks up again.

### Fall (October-November)

I love the fall. As the event season is in full swing, we are constantly in motion. We begin slowly winterizing the gardens, and the whole of New York City is a buzz of activity. However, it can get overwhelming, and every florist begins worrying about the idle winter to come. So, the majority of us end up taking everything we can...much to the detriment of our mental health.

No two days are ever quite the same. My schedule keeps changing due to weather, project adjustments, and efficiency priorities. I also leave gaps for last-minute client needs, serendipitous events, and sales opportunities. If nothing comes up, these holes are filled with creating art, cleaning the studio, writing grants/fellowships, or any of the innumerable things it takes to manage a creative career. Understanding your own hierarchy of priorities is essential in this context.

I run my schedule 6 to 7 days a week, but whenever I can, I give myself at least one full day off a week. This type of schedule keeps the boredom of routine at bay. This kind of life might feel uncertain, even terrifying, for someone who craves predictability. I used to be that way, too. Before I started my business, even the thought of freelancing would give me cold sweats. However, as I've grown as an independent creative, I've also learned to curb these fears with undying faith that:

1)  I can handle whatever comes my way.

2)  I will be provided for by the system/universe/God/divine source.

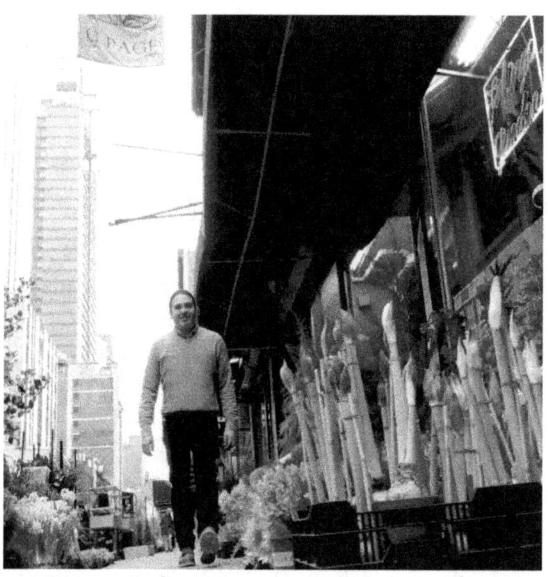

Arriving early at the floral district to shop at the market c. 2021. Photo by S. Bespalov

**Showing Up:**

On the days when inspiration seems elusive and motivation is hard to come by, I still make my way to the studio. I show up as a commitment I've made to myself. I'm paying for the space, yes, but more importantly, it's part of my process. Even if this means sitting idly and waiting for boredom to set in. Why do I wait for the boredom? Because I know well that it invariably breaks the inertia. It prompts me to move, to find something that needs my attention. These moments are integral to self-motivation, a theme we'll explore further in this book.

Even so, I am ever mindful that my phone is a distraction and consciously work to keep it at bay. Instead, I focus on creating something meaningful that sparks a positive feeling and leaves me with a sense of achievement.

**Time to Work:**

This mindfulness of the workflow also applies to how I manage my productive hours. In my twenties, I lived for the late-night creative sprints, those magic hours from 10 p.m. to 2 or 3 a.m. But life has changed. Now, my best work happens between noon and five. It took time to figure that out, and even longer to honor it. But learning when my energy peaks and aligning my schedule with that rhythm has helped me stay focused and make fewer trade-offs with my well-being. It also had much to do with how the client's schedule interacts with my own, and honing and honoring that balance between the practices.

**Building a Power Team:**

At some point in my career, it's unclear where exactly, I realized that the next step in my personal creative evolution was to surround myself with the right experts. As we lay the initial groundwork, it's also crucial to consider finding support while we're working. So much of what it means to show up for ourselves on schedule has to do with reliability and accountability for ourselves, our clients, and our teams. The truth is that no significant achievement can be reached alone, and it is one of the only tangible routes for creating larger achievements.

Learning to hire and work with a team was a vital step in my growth, and a skill honed through trial and error. It has been invaluable. There's an art to assembling a balanced, priority-focused team. It took time and a deliberate investment to find the right people who could fill the necessary roles on my crew. It's also a process I continue to refine.

To clarify, in my business, what I label as 'my team' consists of freelance subcontractors who are experts in floral design, gardening, and fabrication. Alongside them are interns or junior florists, whom I take on when I sense that I am reaching pivotal moments in my business. I then continuously train and mentor them forward. The opportunity to train interns has been one of the most rewarding aspects of running my company. They receive one-on-one guidance, and I get to shape their understanding of how I run my business. Interns are paid a reduced freelance rate for a year, which benefits both parties.

Surprisingly, this training process has become one of the true joys of my business. The contractors I work with are people I've known for years, formally freelanced with, and are either recommended by trusted colleagues or former interns who have grown into fully trained professionals.

Understanding each team member's strengths and weaknesses has been essential for me. This knowledge is invaluable, particularly when we need to break into smaller groups for specific tasks. A common trait I look for in my team members is a strong work ethic paired with a positive spirit. We all participate, help one another, and maintain an open and honest dialogue. This culture has been key to our team's retention and success, and it's why I feel they return year after year.

My projects are typically one-offs, unique to each client's needs, which creates a continual cycle of learning for everyone involved. Each of us learns from the strengths of the others, creating a positive and synergistic experience that elevates the work.

Still, I'm cautious about bringing new people into the fold. The mindset and culture I've developed with my core team are essential to maintaining cohesion. Trustworthiness, honesty, a strong work ethic, the ability to give and receive constructive feedback, and creative problem-solving are all essential for a successful fit. And we will come back to working with the team and vendors later, but it is nice to start off knowing that finding help on our path is a nonnegotiable.

**Replenish the Source:**

I've learned that even with all the help in the world, creativity isn't an endless well. And even though I wholeheartedly embrace my work, if I want to keep drawing from it, I need to refill it.

Sometimes that means stepping away from the everyday work and wandering through an art show, browsing a hardware or art supply store, exploring a new neighborhood, or researching a new hobby. These small detours can spark a wealth of new ideas or may help me view my work from a different angle. In essence, it is replenishing the creative fuel.

> *Side Bar: As I've matured, I've learned to manage new inspiration better. I used to latch onto every new idea and become all consumed by it, as my brain craves new obsessions. Now, I let inspiration flow like water instead of clinging like oil. This change helps me stay curious without risking burnout from short-lived pursuits.*

Finding and maintaining a balance has become even more important post-pandemic. Somewhere in the grind of growing a business and building a brand, I lost sight of the importance of taking a genuine break. And not another to-do list for self-care, but rather an honest, agenda-free day off. Just like a computer entering sleep mode, it's a personal recalibration that ensures everything runs more smoothly when I return.

**Assessing the Recalibration:**

Along the way, I've also stopped believing that hustle is the holy grail. Burnout isn't a badge of honor. I've stopped wearing it like one. Don't get me wrong, I still work hard, probably harder than ever, but I don't come to it from a place of fear or scarcity. When I find myself dragging or resisting, when the ground feels barren and depleted to the core, I pause and check in:

- Am I avoiding giving something its due attention out of fear?
- Do I actually need to rest?
- Or am I spinning out and need to find a new way forward?

Finding the answer is imperative. And if it is rest that is needed, that requires honesty and discipline.

**On Goals:**

One final thought that I would feel remiss in mentioning in this initial chapter, and as we get started, is the importance of setting goals. They have been one of the most grounding practices in my career. I learned this mindset early on through sports and other creative disciplines. Even so, goal-setting isn't the focus of this discussion (entire books are dedicated to it), but I will note that deadlines, structure, and intention are what prevent me from drifting off course. Goals give direction to my work, and a well-planned schedule that balances my ambition and need for rest has been the key to staying on track. I won't elaborate on them further because, for me, what's more important than setting and maintaining goals is creating the routines that enable me to achieve them in the long run.

So, what has this principle of setting a schedule actually done in my life? For one, it's given me more time, real, usable, soul-nourishing time. Because when I'm the one setting my schedule, I also get to decide how it gets used. I get to call the breaks, the breathers, the boundaries. And that is a beautiful, remarkable thing.

It took time to establish a structured schedule that allowed freedom to truly coexist. But once I did, everything changed. I was able to do the work consistently, not perfectly, but consistently. I learned when to call in help, when to double down, and just as importantly, when to walk away and rest. That combination of focus, effort, and restoration has been the initial building block in my career. It's what's made the difference between burnout and longevity. Remember, you don't need to wait for permission; this is truly the best part. You already hold the authority.

**You get to shape your time, and by doing so, you shape your life.**

## Reflections:

- Have you ever allowed the world to dictate how you should operate?

- What does your current schedule reveal about the way you prioritize your time? What patterns emerge? Do they point to something more profound?

- Have you ever felt afloat, or the opposite, so 'in it' that you forgot to come up for air?

# 2

# CREATING SPACE

I remember when my mother was finally getting together her storefront. The excitement, enthusiasm, and jittery joy she had was infectious. She was so proud walking through the storefront when she finally found "The One."

"I know it doesn't look like much now, *hijo...Pero*, look at these windows and all the light! And, *nombre*, we are going to be on the *mero esquina*, the main corner!" Her eyes glowed. You could almost see the dream playing out in real-time, like a movie in her eyes.

"Oh, don't mind the floors, we are going to put in brand new indoor/outdoor carpeting in the main floor area. And, Here...Here, I'm going to have your *Tio* build me a counter in all white for our cash wrap. I'm getting a brand new register, too...an electronic one with a calculator built in! Don't worry, I'll teach you how to use it."

She pointed to an area just to the left of the main door. "Here, we are going to put a brand new triple-wide cooler. So, as people come in, they can see all our fresh roses. I'm getting the big one because you know we are only going to carry long-stemmed roses." The cooler would live across from the cash wrap, where she would be able to see what was in stock as she'd take orders over the phone; she mimed this for me.

"We are going to have a balloon section here." Pointing to the corner next to where the cooler would live. "That's going to be your and your little sister's job when we get busy...I'll show you how to blow them up the right way so you don't pop all my balloons. *Eso duele cuando te pasa*, that hurts when it happens...those mylars are expensive, y *ya sabes* all those little costs add up." My sister and I hated that job, by the way. Luckily, I got my driver's license first so that I could take over delivery duties instead. Not that delivering all those balloon bouquets in a hundred-degree-plus weather in my tiny two-door hand-me-down hatchback car was any better.

"*Y aquí*, and here, your *Tio* is going to put up a lattice wall and an 'old west saloon style' swinging door so I can keep an eye on the customers and separate my work area."

Her work area would be in a quartered-off section, with a back door accessing the gated-off passageway leading to the building's parking area. She had my uncle also construct a simple plywood work table and a gift-wrapping station in her work area.

"In the other room, I can do big displays in my window and change them for all the holidays. We should put a big *Coyote* (our high school mascot) there for homecoming because everyone stops at that light on their way to the high school! Can you paint me one? I'm also going to get lots of plants for that room. We are also going to put up some shelves with plush animals, all sizes, and baggies of candies to let people know we do gift baskets."

She continued in rapid fire, rattling off images to complete the story, "I'm also thinking about putting up a net on the ceiling to hold the balloons that we'll have ready 'to grab and go' when the customer comes in... in case they are in a rush and also for when we get busy during holidays."

With that, the vision for *The Rose Image* was set. This is one of the great things about starting a floral business; she'd always remind me: "You don't need a lot to get started, only a cooler, a register, and a place to work." You can get and maintain everything else as the orders come in.

Experiencing the excitement of my mother achieving her dream of creating a flower shop of her own, one that would fuel her passion, was undeniable. Witnessing this experience firsthand underscored the importance of customizing a creative space from the outset, making sure it reflects our vision and supports our particular workflow.

**My Dream:**

When I was growing up, my dream of having my own artist studio looked quite different. I envisioned an industrial space with tall loft ceilings, open and airy, with 10-foot tall windows or, even better, skylight windows. I wanted a space where the glorious light would filter in and shift at different times of the day, and I could see the light change throughout the year. This was my singular goal after leaving art school, but ultimately, it led only to frustration as I struggled to create work, organize my life, and find myself.

My personal creative spaces have run the gamut. They have included sunrooms, shared studio spaces (both private and open), a leaky, drafty dining room, a second bedroom, a 5-foot-tall, partially exposed, unfinished, spider-ridden basement, and the corner of my NYC studio apartment living room for a time.

The main point is, I've continually found a creative workspace wherever I am. More importantly, my focus has never faltered, and it has always been to continue producing on schedule. Regardless of the situations we may be presented with, it will be necessary, as creatives, to find a space that we can make our own.

Finally, after many years of hard work and searching, I found my own permanent space, and having it is something special. It has become my inner sanctum, a fortress of solitude. My current work studio, at the time of the writing of this book, is a whopping 144 square feet. I do have a 15-

foot ceiling, though. It was initially, and quite <u>literally</u>, a broom closet with an adjoining small room. It took nearly six months to figure out the foundational space and how it could function while still being a place I would be excited to get to daily. I sincerely love and cherish my time in this space. I think visitors pick up on that energy.

Even with its size limitation, we can still produce substantial floral productions/installations, and there are a few factors at play to be able to do so:

1) For our larger projects, we rent auxiliary space within our building to accommodate the overflow.
2) I don't host potential client meetings in my studio (it is my nexus and my incubator). It's much more productive to have these meetings on-site. That's where I sell 'the dream' to the client.
3) Large-scale production happens on-site in the space in which the piece will live. Leaving my studio space open to pre-production and storage.
4) Finally, and most importantly, the crew and I stay efficient and organized. Tools and hard goods return to their given place after use **every time.**

In a micro space, there is a lot of pulling supplies out from their often hidden storage areas, which makes the process a bit more complex. Even so, I've found this to be true in some of the largest warehouse studios where I've freelanced. It may be one of those nuanced peculiarities intrinsically part of operating a business and studio in New York City. Or, maybe it is simply a creative thing in general.

Having your own independent studio space is ideal. But for many, especially newer creatives, that may not be the reality. Don't let this discourage you! As the saying goes, great things come from modest beginnings. I've learned firsthand how frustration and resentment can drain the energy that would be better spent creating. I love what motivational speaker Jim Rohn once said (paraphrased): "Don't complain about all you've got... because that's all you've got!" Or, as my *Abuelita* would say,

# CREATING SPACE

"If you make the most of what you have now, you'll appreciate all the blessings still to come so much more."

Gratitude is healing.

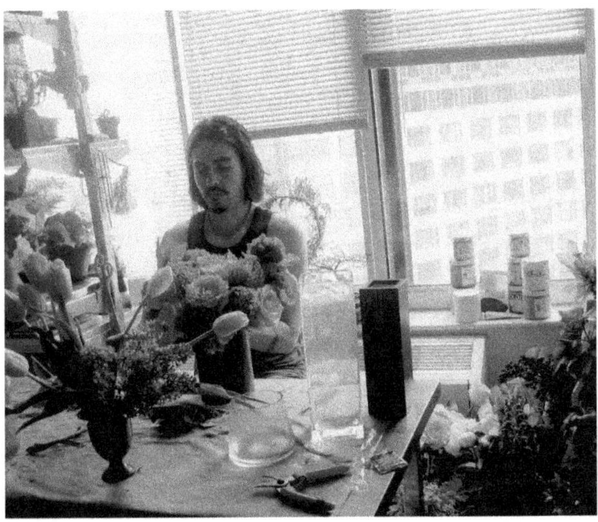

At my home studio in my living room, after I started my business in the spring of 2009. Photo by my wife.

**What I need in a studio space:**

As you read, you'll quickly find two things in this book: I am obsessed with studio spaces and lists. Here are a few accommodations I've found helpful in my artistic and floral creative spaces.

1) Adequate light
2) A solid surface, e.g., a table!
3) A comfortable place to sit or rest
4) A secure place
5) Dry and healthy environment (the dark, dusty, moldy, spider-ridden basement was quickly abandoned)
6) Access to electricity, water, and restrooms
7) Lastly, and maybe most importantly, autonomy

Some of these will be obvious, but if there are readers who are anything like I was in those early days, then it warrants mentioning. There were times, like in that moldy, spider-ridden basement, I was so eager for my own space that I risked my health and safety to keep working. So, yes, it is worth mentioning.

Let's break down these items.

**Lighting and Work Surface:**

Lighting and a tabletop surface will be the backbone of the studio space, even if it's a makeshift one. As you may well know, creativity strikes at all hours of the day. This is when lighting is imperative. In particular, if a project with a deadline is nearing, I might be up late or before sunrise. Having the correct amount of light was also a factor when I was working out of the corner of my tiny NYC apartment late at night. My sleeping spouse did not tolerate the apartment being lit up like JFK Airport at 2:30 am simply because I was suddenly inspired and 'In the Zone,' and rightfully so.

Having a good light source is essential. Invest in daylight-balanced LED bulbs, which reduce eye strain while allowing you to see colors accurately. Don't trust overhead fluorescents alone; supplement with a directional lamp if needed.

As for the work surface, this could be almost anything. I've had pieces of boards laid across egg crates, cheap-o plastic-y folding tables (aka Home Depot Specials), dining room tables, etc. These have all served their purpose. In the end, much of what we do as creatives requires ingenuity.

In my current studio, I use a kitchen island butcher block table purchased at Ikea when I started my business. It was the most significant purchase I made then, costing around $350! Despite what I considered a significant investment at the time, the purchase was justifiable because I knew it would serve me for years.

Along with this, there is a large six-foot-long tool chest workbench combination. I added this tool chest a bit later on, and it's truly been a game-changer for my efficiency and storage! These workbenches also have casters (wheels). This keeps them movable. Lastly, I currently have three 2' x 4' x 5' racks with wheels for storing projects and tools as needed.

**A Place to Rest:**

Next on the list is a place to sit and rest. Don't mistake it, this is an essential element. And something I use daily. Cy Twombly famously sat for hours and then completed a painting in mere minutes. So much of what it means to be a creative or an artist of any kind is rooted in this need to observe. Whether it's people, the projects we are engaged in, or our inner dialogue, a restful place of respite is imperative.

I love looking at images of artists' studios, particularly those of painters. I find them incredibly inspiring. Each artist sets up their space uniquely to suit their workflow. Almost always, along with their art, there is a chair and/or a couch. Everyone has their own speed, and at times, things can get intense, making it important to pause and rest during quieter moments. Additionally, much can be said about observing the work while I calculate the next move or wait for the medium to dry or cure.

**Security:**

Finding a secure space to create our art is important, as what we produce is valuable...at least to us. Additionally, as mentioned, we may need to work late at night, away from the safety of our homes. I acknowledge this with full awareness that my initial budget when I started was near nothing, and I had to accept spaces in straight-up bad neighborhoods. Even if this is the case, it is crucial to prioritize your safety and take necessary measures to protect yourself and your materials. I have heard stories of fellow artists' studios being ransacked during Super Storm Sandy in Red Hook, Brooklyn. Opportunistic criminals are always looking for the best time to strike. Therefore, no matter how affordable a space may be, the cost of losing all your materials to theft or destruction will far outweigh the low rent you pay. A secure space provides peace of mind when you are not around.

At the very least, as my late father would say, "Always remember to lock up" behind yourself, especially when working off hours and going in and out of warehouse buildings. If your workspace is in a shared or high-traffic area, security is a real concern. Safe guard valuables, including expensive tools and specialty floral supplies. When working in a public venue, ensure that your belongings are safely stored. Otherwise, you might find yourself unexpectedly restocking supplies, or even entire racks of stuff, as I did when they mysteriously walked away.

**Keep it Dry and Healthy:**

I think the following two bullet points on the list, finding a dry, healthy environment with access to water and restrooms, are almost a no-brainer...but again, I'm writing this as a special note to my younger self. Damp, moldy areas without proper ventilation are not great for our lungs or work. I've learned to leave a space with these characteristics out of consideration at all costs.

Humidity control is often overlooked but crucial. Excessive moisture causes mold growth. Forced air from the air conditioning or fans can dry out flowers. Even so, air circulation is key; invest in a smaller fan or an air purifier if needed. And remember, standing water is the enemy. Always empty and clean containers at the end of the day to keep your space fresh.

This leads to health; I've learned to make sure that even if I'm in a shed or renting an old building, it is structurally sound, has fire detectors/extinguishers, has access to adequate exits in emergencies, etc. You would not believe some of the nightmare spaces I was presented with in Chicago and NYC when looking for affordable spaces. To put it mildly, in many cases, safety was not the landlord's primary concern.

Lastly, I like to ensure access to heat if I'm in colder climates, potable water, and access to restrooms; also, having a window is lovely. Again, I want to be around to see the fruits of our labor pay off. Sacrificing my health, human needs, and well-being is not what is meant by 'suffering for your craft.'

**Autonomy:**

One of the hardest lessons I learned, especially when I worked from home or in a shared studio, was that our work must become our number one priority. It is hard enough dealing with all the negative self-talk that floods into the average creative mind, let alone having countless others intruding into your space. What it comes down to is respect for ourselves and our art. To protect our time and energy, we must set boundaries. People will interrupt you, assume you're free, or question whether your work is even real work.

No, No, No! Sometimes, you have to be explicit: *THIS IS MY WORK; IT IS A CAREER.* It helps to set clear expectations with the people around you. If you don't, they will set them for you.

**Compromises vs. Non-Negotiables:**

In any shared environment, there will be compromises. But not everything is up for discussion.

### <u>Compromises you might make</u>

1) Wearing headphones to block out noise instead of demanding complete silence or blaring your music in a shared space.
2) Switch out materials if that is a concern. For example, switching from oil paint to acrylics if ventilation is an issue.
3) As mentioned in Chapter One, consider setting specific hours in your schedule for work instead of expecting 24/7 access.

### <u>Non-negotiables</u>

1) Protect and respect your workspace: It's not a communal dumping ground.

2) Set clear boundaries early on. Especially, ones that ward against interruptions during intensely focused projects. If I need two hours, that means two hours.

3) Your work is not a hobby; it's your profession. If people don't take it seriously, that's their problem, not yours.

That said, if you find yourself in any of these situations, have the hard conversations early (and often if need be). The key is to decide what you can bend on and what is essential for your productivity. If you're constantly adjusting to accommodate others, your work will suffer. And no one, no client, no collaborator, will value your time if you don't value it yourself.

A few final thoughts when it comes to this conversation of autonomy, when in floral or art production, I keep the studio clear of unnecessary distractions. And in our building, I take the open/closed-door policy seriously. If my door is closed, I do not want to be disturbed. This sentiment gets explicitly amplified when referring to my art process; I know I only have time in my life to create an 'x' number of pieces. So, I take my studio time seriously and detest interruptions when fully engaged in a new art piece.

This is different when discussing florists' work because there is more leeway during repetitive tasks, allowing time for idle chats, conversation, and gossip.

**Everything is slowly dying from the moment we obtain it... Work with a sense of urgency.**

Flowers fade, materials degrade, and ideas slip away if we don't act on them. Everything is slowly dying from the moment we obtain it. So, work with a sense of urgency. This point is so essential that I taped this phrase above one of my studio doors, because we are often up against the clock during production, and more importantly, because it applies to life in general. You don't need perfect conditions. You simply need to start. And when focused attention is required, there is no time for idle conversation. This doesn't mean I rush my crew to their breaking point, but I expect their acute focus if we are on a schedule.

Why is there so much pressure when it comes to my studio time? Whether up against a deadline or focused on a new series of works, I know the Pareto Principle is at play. Commonly, this is known as the 80/20 rule, which states that approximately 80% of consequences come from 20% of actions. I see this everywhere in my practice and realize it is within that short window of focused attention on which so much rides.

**Insurance:**

And finally, a crucial but often overlooked element of maintaining a studio or event-based business: Insurance. During the early steps of organizing for an event or, in this case, signing a Renter's Agreement for a studio workspace, I like to get all my Certificate of Insurance (COI) and Worker's Compensation (WC) forms submitted for approval. Each space or venue will have its requirements and how they'd like these forms submitted. If you already have yearly coverage, this is a simple process, and most insurance companies allow you to request COI forms instantaneously online. If you are starting and only handle a handful of events a year, you may want to purchase coverage *a la carte*.

Either way, you'll want to request a "Sample COI" form from the venue or building. The sample COIs provide the exact wording you'll need to have on your policy. <u>Do Not Fight</u> this process. <u>Get it done as early as possible</u>. Yes, it will be another EXPENSIVE expense, but there is no way around it if your building or the venue you're working in requires it. Honestly, getting into long-winded negotiations may make you look unprofessional (this comes from experience in those early days of running my business). Also, the insurance is there for your protection as well. We put a lot of effort into building our business, and it is paramount to protect our investments at all times.

**STUDIO LIFE, ODDS AND ENDS:**

- As much as possible, I am constantly focused on staying organized, especially when working in tight quarters. This has helped me keep my tools handy and ready to use at a moment's notice.

- Regarding tools, I started collecting them slowly and acquired specific, specialized tools only when needed, borrowing and renting whenever appropriate.

- When I moved into my current studio, I refused to pay the upcharge for commercial phone service, which is needed to acquire WiFi. This has now become a great way to keep studio costs down and remove unnecessary distractions, keeping my studio time to just that, studio time, not screen time. Perhaps this is something to consider in a world where being disconnected is a new luxury.

- I like to leave paper (or a notepad) and a pen out; I never know when a solution to a problem or question will suddenly pop into my head. Usually, this happens to me when I do a little task like sweeping up or wiping down the table tops...So, I've learned to trick my mind by doing these mindless tasks to force the subconscious to push out these solutions, which it's been figuring out behind the scenes.

- I replace supplies <u>only</u> in order of importance or when NEEDED (there is a vital difference between needs and wants), especially when I am on a strict budget. This one is meant for all those sketchbook hoarders, myself included.

- I've taken a page from Mr. Rogers and keep an extra pair of shoes around. My practice involves standing on my feet most of the time, and switching out shoes at the tail end of my day helps keep me productive and energized. A mentor taught me this one.

- Storage is usually a hurdle, especially in a studio the size of mine. I've found that clearly labeled containers/totes/boxes work well. If a box hasn't been used in a year, it gets donated. Usually, these go to Materials for the Arts, a resource for artistic supplies/materials for New York City Schools. This keeps my storage manageable, helps my community, and is a reasonable tax deduction.

- I'm not afraid to have fun, quirky elements that are nonsensical or make me smile around my studio spaces. Some of the most celebrated creative spaces I've had the privilege to visit also use this practice. They almost all keep interesting personal chatzkeis in their spaces to lighten up their otherwise deadly serious office.

- Even on the busiest days and during the most involved projects, it is rare that I do not find a few extra moments to straighten up as much as possible before I lock up. There is this phenomenal psychological boost I get the next time I head into my space, knowing I am starting the day with a clean slate.

- I constantly have my renter's agreement in my mind. There is no sense in losing a deposit due to damaged floors when I can cover this situation by simply laying down a painter's drop cloth. Likewise, I've often avoided punching holes in the walls by utilizing a table or an easel. I've even used wood fiber soundboard panels as oversized tackboards in the past.

- Lastly, I allow myself to enjoy my space. It doesn't have to be only my place of work. Because I am there so much, I've made a conscious effort to make it a place I yearn to return to. I am tremendously grateful and humbled by the privilege of having a Manhattan-based studio....so yes, I allow myself time to enjoy the space itself. Sometimes, it is enough for me to sit and enjoy the quiet contemplation of my 18-year-old bonsai in my windowless studio indoor garden.

## Reflections:

– Have you ever felt guilty in claiming the space to create, to simply be?

– What shame or self-judgment have you carried for not having the 'perfect' workspace?

– What accommodations are on your list?

– What are your non-negotiables?

# 3

# THE SKILLS

Raised on the ranch and having a naturally inquisitive mind, it was a real challenge. We had little access to learning materials. Remember, this was a time before computers or the internet. In our little town of Alice, we did have a small public library, which I loved. It's still around and is designed in the 70s Mid-century style, which was one of the only notable architectural styles I was exposed to as a child. The library being in town was inconvenient for my parents to get to every time I had questions, because of the 15-mile drive into town.

Eventually, my mother put some money together and got the family a set of encyclopedias. I can probably say that of all the stuff I was blessed to have grown up with, that set of books might have made the most significant difference in how my life has been shaped. The books themselves were great, but my mother's greatest gift to us was making us <u>learn how to learn on our own</u>.

After she gave us those volumes, every time we had a nagging question, her usual response was, "*Aaughh!! Pues*, Look it Up!" We heard it so often from her that my sisters and I started joking and taunting each other about it... "Look it Up! Look it Up!" We would teasingly say it in that playful 'na-na na-na boo-boo' tone. But in doing so, my mother helped us improve our reading skills and taught us a valuable lesson about the importance of finding a self-reliant solution through research. Thank you, Mom!

> *Fun fact: there is a song from the '80s or maybe early '90s about encyclopedias called "Look it up!"...and well, you can look it up on the tiny supercomputer smartphone in your pocket.*

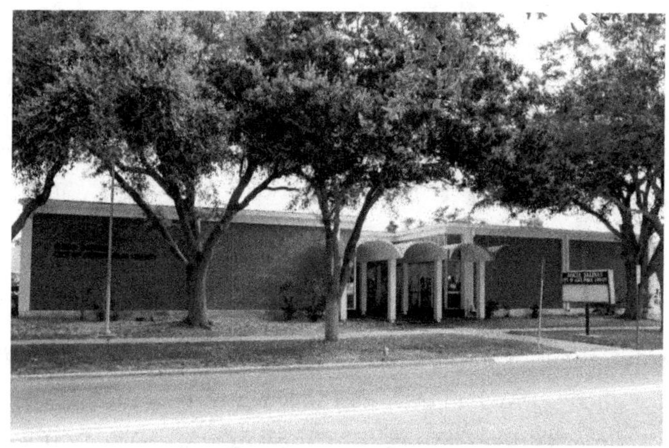

Alicia Salazar City of Alice Public Library. Photo by me.

Long before I set foot in a gallery, my mother's gift laid the groundwork for an ever-expanding mindset for developing skills and continued self-learning. Years later, as an artist, I realized the lessons from those volumes mattered far more than the movie version's story of being 'discovered' and the long road that involves stacking wins and skills, which are almost a requirement on the journey of creatives.

In this chapter, we get into the grit of the matter of acquiring skills. How they stack and serve. Dismantling illusions and narratives, and realizing when we must find experts and where our personal boundaries lie.

**Finding a Mentor:**

If you ever get the chance in life, as I did, to be mentored by someone, it could be a crucial turning point in your career. I was blessed to have my mother, who was highly forthcoming about running the business and its finances. She never sugar-coated the situation. She was quick to explain why this or that was important because having someone say, "Just because!" Doesn't teach you anything about life.

I didn't realize how much I had picked up from her by simply hanging around her flower shop until I started working at a flower shop in Chicago. This is when I slowly realized all the knowledge and experience I had gained. It gave me a huge leg up. Even something as small as professionally answering the phone and taking an order without being too nervous. I will admit, however, that in those early days in Chicago, I was constantly being corrected because my grammar wasn't proper for the high-end clientele we were servicing, but the confidence was there. I'd also learned from her that there will always be something that needs to get done in a flower shop. Whether that's watering or cleaning plants, cleaning buckets and vases, or condensing the cooler, the tasks are endless.

Over the years, I've been lucky to cross paths with some legendary designers, who in time have become quiet mentors, who've shaped me in ways they probably don't even know. I never miss a chance to ask them questions. Not the surface-level stuff, but the real questions:

- What keeps you going?
- What do you wish you'd known?
- What do you let go of now that you didn't before?

Some of the most promising students and interns I've instructed share that same instinct. They know when to listen, when to ask, and how to stay curious without overstepping. It's often a subtle indicator that they're going to make it.

A few reminders: timing matters, so ask with respect, and always keep it professional. People can sense intention, and when it's earnest, when you're not just mining them for secrets, they'll often give more than you expect. Little gold nuggets you can pocket and carry forward. Wisdom swept up from the floor of someone else's lived experience.

**In gardening and floral design, I've learned that 80% of the work is cleaning shit up. Get good at using a broom.**

I love this metaphor because it's so universal. And before I had any true skills to fall back on, I learned to use a broom, because life is messy, and creating is even messier. No matter how high up the ladder you go, whether you're a master florist, a gallery artist, or the party planner of a six-figure event, sooner or later, you're going to be holding a broom. There's something humble and almost sacred in the act. The floor might not stay clean for long, but it's that quiet act of restoring order after chaos that matters.

In floristry, your ability to clean up is a reflection of your professionalism, making it more than just another chore. And for some artists, that's a tough truth. I've noticed we tend to fall into two artistic camps: additive or subtractive. The adders build complexity, layer on texture, and embrace the beautiful chaos in a series of layered stages. The subtractors carve away, pare things down, find the form that hides inside. Each style has its own tolerance for disorder. But make no mistake: no matter your process, the mess will come. The question then becomes, what do you do with it?

The florist who trained me was a subtractive artist. He'd tear through stems of florals and foliage, leaving the floor looking like a tornado had passed through the shop. And then, in the middle of it all, he'd often bend down, pick up a scrap of something fragile, and say, "You have to save these bits, Juan. Waste not, want not." There was order and attention in his seemingly manic making...even if I was often the one left carrying the broom.

In my studio, I have my own saying: "No, your momma doesn't work here." (Even if she does.) We clean up after ourselves and take responsibility for the studio space. This goes far beyond just the physical. As mature artists, we also have to learn to sweep the clutter from our minds, habits, and egos.

**Picking Up Skills, Gradually:**

Clearing out bad habits often starts with learning new ways of being, and while I value all learning, my relationship with traditional education is complicated and has been marked by frustration. Even so, I am always on the lookout for new techniques, courses of action, systems of organization/planning, trades, or ways of effective communication and listening.

Almost all skills can be improved or expanded, and it's quite rare for them to diminish or be lost completely. Taking the time to learn more will definitely be worth it, even if the results aren't always immediate or obvious. For example, my personal interests have often guided me to acquire new skills, which I have then utilized to develop innovative systems that enhance our approach and methods.

Continuing education courses have been one of the greatest gifts I have given to myself. A few of these courses have included:

- Welding
- Woodworking
- Sculpture
- Figure painting in oils
- Podcasting
- Ceramics and pottery
- Laboratory techniques in BioArt

These courses and studies have profoundly influenced my path in some interesting ways, for example:

**Painting** → Developed my eye for color and the patience for long-focused projects.

**Sculpture and Welding** → Taught me construction and how to understand and manage my floral mechanics.

**Figure Painting** → Taught me about proportions, how to break the complex into simple shapes, and how light plays and interacts with these shapes all around us.

**Podcasting** → Gave me confidence to hear my voice, organize my thoughts, and devise scripts.

**Ceramics and Pottery** → Got me used to feeling when something was right with my hands and not necessarily my eyes.

**Bonsai** → Showed me how to create presence, balance, and movement from simple branches.

And as this list could go on for some length, I'll end it here. The point is that all these have helped my floral design directly and tremendously. They've also made me much better at the varying degrees of editing... which is one skill I'm constantly working on. I cannot overstate how grateful I am for the skills I have picked up over the years. So, keep learning, and when you can, take a class, even if it's only an online tutorial. Because if we never learn to sharpen our own mental swords, we begin taking what we are being sold at face value. And that is all too often someone else's myth.

**No Straight Lines, Only Layers:**

Let's be honest, many of us didn't grow up learning about a mindset that really shapes long-term success, especially one built on gradually developing skills. Even fewer of us got to see artists thriving.

We saw the myth: the one where someone with talent is discovered, plucked out of obscurity or the gutter, by luck, fate, or a well-connected stranger. A tight story with a clean trajectory. And it often looked like make the work, show the work, get spotted, get signed, get paid. The big cut scene into the white box gallery, the agent nervously watching, in the hot lights, as the gallery fills with champagne-sipping buyers.

It's the version of success I once believed, too. It's the story we're all sold, in movies, in media, even by well-meaning family and friends.

"Did you get your big break yet?"

"Are you famous?"

"Is the work in a gallery?"

They mean well. But underneath those questions lies a belief that artistic success follows a clear and glamorous path. That if you haven't "made it," it's because you're not good enough, fast enough, strategic enough. And it is fiction.

The reality is more cutthroat, more layered. And sadly, it isn't always about the quality of the work. Often, it's about the narrative wrapped around the artist. Tropes get sold more than truth. And the actual money is not made in the first sale. That comes in the secondary market of auctions and resales, where collectors and investors profit, while the artist, more often than not, sees little. The artist becomes the product, not the work. This isn't bitter hyperbole. In the real art world, work gets passed around like a blue-chip stock, and the artist's name is what needs to be protected from any impending bubble crash.

I say all this not to discourage you. This is to clear the air. Because if you know what you're walking into, you can walk in prepared. Not jaded... prepared. You then decide what games you want to play, or don't. But you can't be in it if you don't even know the rules or the board.

This also means finally rejecting the myth that there's one clean, glamorous road to success. There isn't. There's only the one you make by continuing to show up when no one is watching, and the praise that arrives is quiet when the doubt is louder than the inspiration.

It means deep devotion to the practice itself. Learning what you don't yet know. Sharpening your tools. Stacking your skills like bricks to build something sustainable. That process of acquiring new skills, applying them, and evolving is what's real.

Our job as creatives isn't to replicate someone else's story. Our job is to dismantle myths and build something more honest in their place.

And yes, as the work grows, you'll hit limits. That's normal. No one excels at everything. That's when you learn to ask for help, to collaborate, to call in the specialists. Creating truly monumental work that lasts is never a solo effort.

**Calling in the Specialist:**

Knowing the board doesn't mean you won't sometimes play too many roles at once. It took many hard learned lessons and season after season, where I nearly wore myself out trying to do it all alone. So, while acquiring new skills is all-important on our paths, we must eventually acknowledge our limitations as our projects expand. This is especially true as we hit roadblocks where our skills hold us back. From past experiences, I know that no one can do or should be expected to excel at everything. This took a long time to learn, and it is one of those realizations that would have been invaluable to my younger self. I used to believe that I had to conquer every task single-handedly. Admittedly, at times, I still do.

Delegation and collaboration are invaluable when tasks are beyond my expertise. Learning how and when to seek help is not a sign of weakness, as I once thought. By hiring specialists, I free up valuable time to focus on what I do best. This pushes our projects forward efficiently. Understanding how to harness this power can create a dynamic synergy within a business.

This lesson is hard to swallow, especially for a creative, 'do-it-yourself' type like myself. However, its beauty and complexity came to light when I was a freelancer in the ultra-luxury event industry. The luxury designers I worked for would hire numerous subcontractors who were highly specialized in each aspect of the event installation.

In the world of ultra-luxury events, there are tent people and people to drape those tents. There is usually a separate sound and lighting company. There are custom dance floor people, furniture rental companies, plant rental companies, fabricators, and carpenters for all those custom touches. I've seen seamstresses contracted to create specialized pillows for seating areas or draped linen tablecloths. Neon-sign specialists and people who work singularly on stage setups. This doesn't even begin to include the photographers, videographers, A-list entertainers, DJs, bands, cellists, and dancers. Yes, dancers, you know, to motivate the guests to dance and entertain. Silkscreen artists for on-site custom shirts, photo booth operators, face painters, sound producers, the all-important PR company, catering and staffing, valets, security, gardeners, custodians to prep the grounds and maintain ultra-luxury portable bathrooms and lounges...etc. Etc.

Regarding finding contractors, if you need to hire rental companies, prop vendors, and fabricators, this should become a constant part of your research practice. From the day I started my business, I slowly began collecting these contacts and am constantly searching for additional options. This process expands my network and fosters a sense of community and support within the event industry. If you anticipate that this will be part of your services but currently lack the necessary connections, a great place to begin is by asking your network of florists for recommendations. If you don't know anyone else in the industry, your local wholesalers may also be a good starting point.

**A Man of Many Hats:**

Before I truly understood how to call in experts, or even what that meant, I was deep in the weeds doing everything myself. I still wrestle with that impulse. But one story, early on, taught me just how deeply that instinct ran...

One day, during a freelancing gig, one of the crews I was working with was being transported to the Hamptons for one of these luxury events, and I was fortunate enough to ride with the company's owner. Of course, I started interviewing him.

I started, "I love the new photos you recently added to your website. Was that easy to do?". His response was, "Yeah...I guess.". I continued to pick his brain, "How were you able to get the lighting so nice and achieve those beautiful backlit shots with the sun pouring in so nicely, highlighting those impeccable white cosmos?" He, in a bit of a curt tone, "We hired a photographer, and they produced the photoshoot in the studio. We then sent those photos off to the website designer.”

I quickly retorted, “Ah, that makes sense.” Cut to me staring vacantly out the window for the remainder of the two and a half hour ride to the Hamptons.

So naive! Here, I thought everyone was like me, wearing every hat imaginable and overly controlling every aspect of the creative process.

See, at the time, I was also trying to put together my first business website. I’m working to get rid of that word, *trying*, from my vocabulary, but here, it fits. I was fumbling my way through taking photos of my floral arrangements with a little point-and-shoot camera. The best I could afford at the time was one of those basic models with an automatic mode, a simple video feature with no stabilization, and a manual mode that didn’t support all the necessary functions. It didn’t really matter because I knew nothing about photography. I did know how to frame up a shot, but then I’d just point, click, and hope.

Editing those images was another mess, entirely. I had no real software, only whatever clunky tool came bundled with the camera. I recall being able to only crop, adjust the brightness, and maybe boost the contrast a touch. And then, with great pride and zero technical experience, I’d upload them to a website I had stitched together myself, on a free beta version of WordPress. It was basically all trial, but mostly error. I had no programming knowledge, no design sensibility when it came to the digital world. You can imagine the final product: not exactly polished. But it existed. I made it.

So, yes, all this talk about calling in experts and acquiring the right skills, please take it with a grain of salt. I don’t always take my own advice. I still fall into the trap of doing it all myself. I still struggle to delegate or ask for help. Even now, writing this, I feel the rawness of that truth. There’s a certain safety in doing everything solo; it gives the illusion of control. And frankly, I love the challenge. I get high off learning something new, proving I can figure it out. But if I’m being honest, that resistance to letting anyone else in is a wound. A response shaped by earlier versions of me, one that learned to rely only on myself. There’s more to say about that, and we'll get to it later. For now, let's name it and leave it open.

Skill-building in a creative practice isn't a straight path. For me, it's been mostly self-taught, patched together with a stubborn resourcefulness. As a kid, I read those encyclopedias like they were novels. Later, I learned to seek out people who knew more than I did, asking questions, taking classes, and staying curious. Some skills I acquired out of necessity, while others simply lit a spark in me. Actual progress was never fast. Over time, every rough attempt and hard-earned lesson contributed to shaping the foundation I build upon today. Hell, it's how this book has come together as well, if we are being 100% honest.

Which drives home the point that even the rough beginnings matter; they're proof we had the courage to start. So, keep learning, making, and showing up. Ultimately, the skills we acquire serve as the vehicles that help us on the long road to achieving our goals. And, when all else fails, go on and grab a broom...especially before the client arrives!

---

# Reflections:

- How does nostalgia show up in your practice? Does it inspire or limit you?

- What's been your relationship with education, formal or informal?

- What have your hands taught you that your words never could?

- Are you building skills as a way to advance the practice, or using it to hide behind and distract from something deeper?

# 4

# WHY

"Does this ever get easier?" I asked, only half-joking, as I passed a mentor on the stairs in my studio building, sweat clinging to my back, my lungs doing their best to catch up..

He didn't miss a beat. "No," he said.

I smiled and laughed, but inside, I thought, "Jesus. Then what the hell is the point?"

That was one of those days that tests our resolve and has us questioning the reason for it all. I was tired, overwhelmed, and slowly unraveling. The work had pushed me past my edge again, and the list of things I didn't know felt like it was doubling by the hour.

By the time I made it to my bench in the studio, I was spiraling: "What am I even doing? Am I cut out for this? Is this what the rest of my life is supposed to feel like?"

And just as I was starting to drown in that inner doubt, a memory surfaced, uninvited but undeniable. A moment I hadn't thought about in years.

**Discovering My WHY:**

After I dropped out of art school, cliché, I know, I kept painting while working a retail job to pay the rent. My studio was the empty dining room of a beat-up apartment on Chicago's west side. It was drafty, in a rough neighborhood, and barely held together, but the rent was cheap, and the landlady didn't mind paint on the floors or more holes in the walls. It wasn't perfect, but it was mine. I'd stay up all night in there, painting like my life depended on it.

Eventually, my artist friend and I organized a show in a sleek restaurant-gallery in Wicker Park. A world apart from where I lived, but I invited the crew from my retail job anyway.

At the time, I worked in the MTV department of the new Viacom flagship megastore on the Magnificent Mile, a place that didn't last long, but for a minute, felt like the center of something. Everyone there had an edge. We thought we were so cool...too cool for school, as they used to say.

To my surprise, almost everyone came. Toward the end of the night, one of the guys from work, someone I barely knew, the quiet kind, magnetic but distant, approached me.

"I don't usually go to art shows anymore," he said.

I raised an eyebrow. "Okay..."

He hesitated. "I used to paint. But I haven't touched my brushes in years."

Then he stared me deep in the eyes, and said, with a kind of composed certainty: "Your art has inspired me. Thank you. Truly."

"I think I'm going to dig out my paints from under the bed."

To this day, that moment lives in me. Because somehow, simply by doing what I loved, I helped someone else remember what they loved. Nothing sold that night, but I went home with something better; the beginning of an answer to a question I hadn't fully asked until then: "Why am I doing this?"

Which brings me back to me, sitting in my flower studio, chin in my palms, wondering what the hell it was all for, when that memory, and the emotions of that night, came rushing back. It was so simple: To Inspire.

In the days that followed, I pulled out an old painted panel I'd kept in storage, and found a frame my artist friend, the same one I'd shared that show with, had once gifted me. On the panel, I wrote "To Inspire" in gold leaf.

It's still the greatest compliment I can imagine, especially coming from one creative to another.

I hung the piece above my coat rack in the studio. So now, every time I walk in, I'm met with humility, gratitude, and a clear vision of why I'm there.

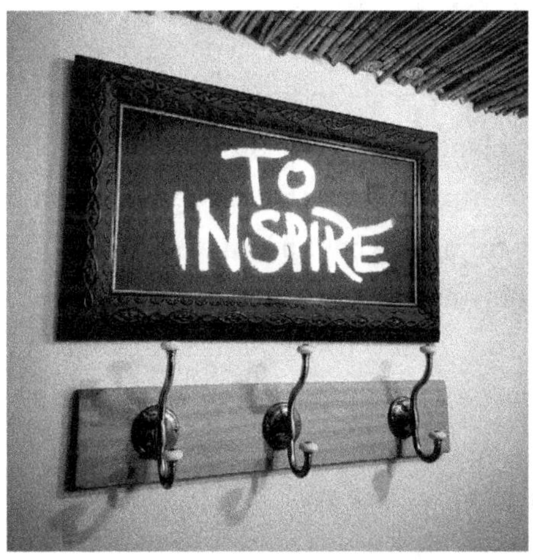


*To Inspire*, gold leaf panel, frame made by a dear friend and collaborator from my first duo show in Chicago. Photo by me.

***Side Note:*** *The framed "To Inspire" piece once had something else scrawled on it in chalk: "Keep It Simple, Stupid!" Which, honestly, is also solid advice when starting a creative business.*

That memory didn't just remind me why I do this work; it realigned me. It snapped something back into place, both emotionally and fundamentally. To Inspire. I had said it so many times, but in that moment, I felt it again. Raw and real.

But truthfully, knowing your "why" is one thing. Living it, building something from it, is another. That spark of inspiration has to be anchored to something steady. Otherwise, it burns out under the weight of fatigue, stress, or doubt.

That realization took me back, back to the beginning, when I was just starting to figure out what this business would be. I didn't have a language for it yet, no neat mission statement or clearly outlined set of values. Forget about a formal business plan. I was just doing whatever I could to survive. Still, a new direction was forming.

It reminded me of the process of pruning a young shrub. I always start with careful edits made with the future of the plant in mind. Making initial bold, rough cuts, I then wait a season, giving the plant time to heal and to acclimate. Later, I begin to fine-tune slowly, cutting back what no longer serves the plant. This slow process helps its strongest form to emerge. Careful pruning of growth requires discipline, vision, restraint, and the courage to cut back what no longer serves.

That's what this next stretch of my journey was about. It was a time for making room for clarity. I needed a clear understanding of what I stood for, what I needed to protect, and what I had to let go of in my life.

**Creating My Mission Statement:**

When I was crafting a vision for my business, I started by clarifying my core beliefs. These values became the foundation of my mission statement. Having this mission gives me a steady hand guiding me to stay true to what matters most in my business. Although I have made minor adjustments to the wording over the years, the core message remains the same. Today, it reads as follows:

> *At Villanueva Designs, we provide unique and innovatively designed biophilic floral works specifically created for the individual needs of our clients, with the uncompromised focus of bringing beauty into their homes and lives.*

What can I point out here? Well, to start, it took a lot of time to find the exact words to concisely express the intent of my business in a single sentence. In a way, I could highlight the three main concepts of our company: We create innovative botanical works for our clients with the intention of spreading beauty. It sounds simple enough, but creating this mission statement took months, and as I stated, it is still in evolution.

**The Vision:**

First, I needed to determine my intention to start a business. This was an arduous task. I knew I wanted to create a company focused on serving the client's needs in varied botanical forms, whether with floral arrangements, installations, indoor plants, garden maintenance, or any number of florist practices. I also knew I <u>did not</u> want to take on the duties of a flower shop, meaning having the business be solely based on daily orders from the general public. It was as crucial for me to know what I want as it was to understand what I did not. Both were powerful in discovering my true vision.

My systematic approach gave me a concise vision for the business, which focused on my relationship with my private clients. Later, this private client-based model helped inform the practices I used in my B2B (business-to-business) interactions. Even so, the original business model has remained the same at its core, enabling me to add services to the business.

> **Important Note:** <u>*First and foremost, the work must be interesting to me and*</u> **<u>THEN</u>** <u>*the client.*</u> **Do not take this statement lightly.** *It is fundamental to the entire creative process.*

From the beginning, I've viewed each floral piece as a small sculpture (sometimes grand). Admittedly, this perspective was inspired by advice from the floral mentor I mentioned earlier, long before I entered the world of private client floral design. At that time, I was working for him and particularly nervous about messing up a customer's expensive order, and I remember he said to me, "Juan, think of them as sculptures, and you'll be fine." He was right.

So, with my intentions clarified, I soft-launched my company in 2008, hoping to bring my floral sculptures to a handful of private clients. It was a beginning that came with no fanfare, no huge announcements, and no blueprint, just a clear desire to create work that felt honest and alive.

But clarity of vision doesn't make the path easy. Building a business, pursuing art, or simply living a life with integrity is demanding. What helped me stay grounded through it all was regularly checking in with myself to clarify where I was headed and why I was heading there.

That kind of reflection became part of my discipline. I asked myself often:

- What still feels true?
- What needs to evolve?
- What am I working toward now?

Staying connected to those questions, along the way, has become its own form of self-respect. It helps me course-correct, refine, and recommit.

Knowing my 'why' gave me a compass and purpose. Something I could return to in hard moments, to help me discern which challenges were worth meeting and which I could release, prune away.

Your core driver might look completely different. It should. But during the long, challenging days when doubt starts to sneak in and work feels tougher than the initial joy that inspired it, having something tangible to lean into is indispensable.

My truth, *To Inspire*, doesn't promise ease. But it does offer direction, and it reminds me that even the smallest acts of sincere creation can ripple further than we know. That clarity keeps me steady, especially when everything else feels uncertain.

But even the clearest sense of purpose isn't enough on its own. It has to be protected, guarded, and respected. The benefits of working through these personal values, knowing your why, and creating a mission statement may very well be something that carries you if you ever find yourself chin in hand, wondering what it's all for.

---

## Reflections:

– Has defining your "why" become a pillar in your work?

– Have you considered developing your own personal creative mission statement? What's in it?

– What questions do you reflect on, and keep you connected to self-respect?

# 5

# THE CREATIVE PROCESS

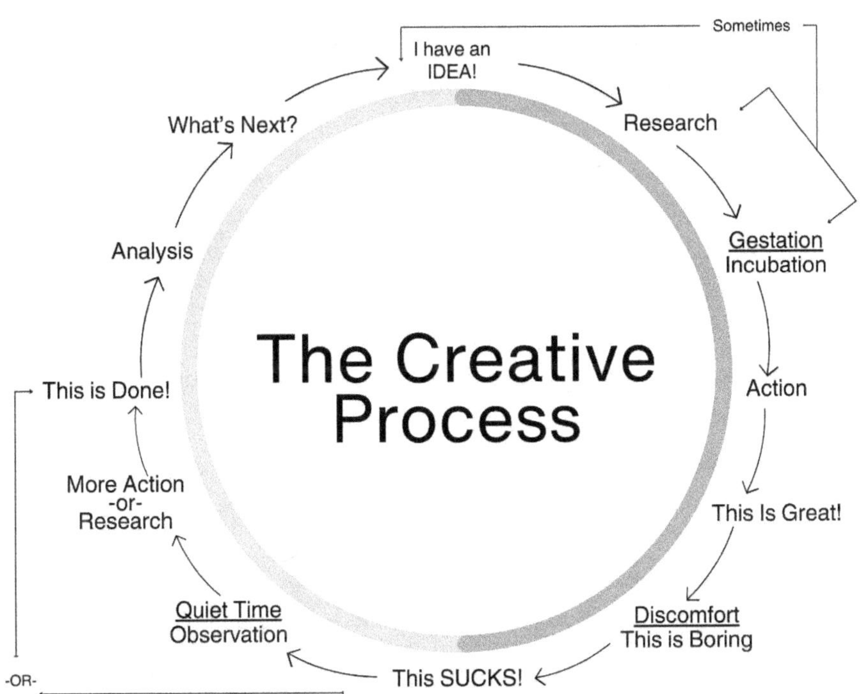


At the heart of it all is the creative process.

In this chapter, I'll walk you through the creative process I use almost daily in my inter-/multidisciplinary artistic practice. So, what exactly is the creative process? It's a set of steps I follow in pursuing a creative goal, whether that's creating a painting, organizing an event, or solving a complex problem. I love the diagram I've included because it accurately reflects the process about 98% of the time.

We've already discussed the importance of having a clear vision for both art and career. Now, I want to introduce the emotions, thoughts, and challenges that tend to arise along the way. This process won't do anything for you, but it will make you aware of what to expect at different stages. When things feel uncertain, I remind myself to trust the process.

I was first introduced to this concept by my freshman high school art teacher in Calallen, Texas. I wish I could remember his name because he was a phenomenal instructor; tough, but he pulled the best out of his students. He taught the creative process through rigid drawing exercises: drawing without looking at the paper, keeping the pencil on the page at all times. If he caught you drawing what you pictured rather than what you saw, he'd snatch up your paper, crumple it, and toss it in the trash. Can you imagine that happening today? (That is, if we still had art in schools, but that's another book.)

His goal was to break down our habitual ways of seeing and thinking, forcing us to truly observe. He even timed these exercises so he could pinpoint exactly where we'd struggle most. That's how predictable this process can be.

**Before we dive deeper into it, feel free to jump to the sections that interest you and return as needed. There's no wrong way to explore it.**

**The Idea:**

It all starts with an idea... or does it? That initial spark of insight seems to come from somewhere deep in the imagination. I can't always pinpoint exactly where. Sometimes, ideas strike out of nowhere, and often at the most random times. Other times, they need to be coaxed out and nurtured through research, observation, or by immersing ourselves in other art. Part of being a professional creative means becoming a conduit for ideas to pass through. And the only way to do that is by showing up and doing the work.

This is why keeping a pen and notepad (or, let's be real, a smartphone) nearby can be really useful. Inspiration doesn't always arrive when it's convenient, and ideas have a habit of slipping away as quickly as they appear. I used to experience vivid ideas for paintings, and I'd quickly need to jump into a quick thumbnail sketch to capture them. These days, since I'm constantly making, the ideas flow in more naturally. They no longer feel like sudden bursts but rather a steady undercurrent.

Interestingly, I've also found that this stage isn't always a clear-cut "first step" in the process. Often, it blends seamlessly into the next phase. At this point in my career, I'm frequently working within constraints: budgets, deadlines, and client expectations. For example, if I'm tasked with organizing a large floral event or installation, I might skip right past this 'idea' stage and dive into research mode.

But whether your idea is fully formed or still taking shape, this is generally where it all begins. That said, as you'll see in the diagram, the creative process is a circle for a reason. We're rarely moving through it in a neat, linear fashion. More often than not, we're cycling through different stages. Sometimes several at once while juggling multiple projects.

**Research:**

I'll be honest: when I was younger, I hated research. I wanted to skip straight to the making. Those dreaded research papers in writing class were pure torture. However, research has now become the backbone of my creative practice. It's where that initial spark of an idea starts to take shape and gain clarity.

For floral event projects, my research usually starts with understanding the group or organization I'm working with. If it's a nonprofit, I check their website for recent campaigns. What imagery are they using? What's the color palette? Are the themes playful or more serious? Where in the world are their visuals sourced from? These clues help shape my creative approach. Sometimes, a client provides a mood board, which can serve as a shortcut to staying on-brand.

I also make it a priority to visit the venue whenever creating site-specific installations. As I briefly mentioned earlier, when I started out, I imagined meeting clients in my perfectly curated studio, complete with rattan chairs and a shabby-chic seating area. That never happened. Instead, I quickly realized that a site visit is invaluable. Seeing the space in person allows me to visualize how floral treatments can be integrated, how the lighting interacts with the surroundings, and where key focal points should be. It's a much more dynamic and intuitive process than staring at a floor plan.

Brainstorming naturally happens in tandem with research. For me, this stage is fluid. I don't map out every thought in a whole 'cloud-form' diagram thing. Instead, I work through ideas by talking them out, usually with my team. We toss around concepts, refine them, and narrow them down to two or three strong directions. Since I've built a culture of open communication, my crew has a say in how we execute ideas, creating a sense of ownership and fluid teamwork.

These conversations also lead us into the nuts and bolts, materials, labor needs, timelines, and yes, the budget. It might sound counterintuitive, but this is still a deeply creative part of the process. Knowing our numbers sharpens the vision. It sets the boundaries we must push against, which often leads to more resourceful, more imaginative solutions. Constraints refine our creativity when held with intention.

From there, I start gathering materials and sourcing items for samples. This part excites me. I look at colors, textures, and forms, thinking about how to use them in unexpected ways. How does the materiality of an object contribute to the story I want to tell? I build narratives through subtle references, layering meaning into each composition. To engage the viewer, I often start with something exquisite but familiar. An impeccable tulip or a bold orchid, for example, may invite a closer look. Some people will only see the obvious and might think, "Meh, pretty flower," and move on. That's fine. They aren't my audience.

Sometimes, the idea itself is born from research. Many of my fine art pieces have started with a single word or concept that lodged itself in my brain, demanding exploration. This is where my hyperfocus kicks in. A prime example? My residency at the School of Visual Arts in Interdisciplinary Practices in Bio-Art. I spent most of my time there deeply immersed in research, which, in turn, generated the work I created.

Research isn't limited to books or websites. It happens everywhere, walking through a different neighborhood, flipping through magazines, visiting galleries, and museums. These simple acts spark new ideas. As creatives, we are always researching, whether we realize it or not. It's how we grow.

**Gestation:**

At this point, you might feel like it's time for a break...well, exactly. After all that research, there's a necessary incubation period. Some ideas need time. This isn't procrastination; procrastination is knowing you should act but choosing not to. Gestation is different. It's about waiting for the right course of action to reveal itself. Like planting tulip bulbs in the fall, some ideas need time to rest before they bloom.

As creatives, we know this instinctively. During my Bio-Art residency, I heard stories about lab techs who worked with artists and struggled to understand this concept.

Wait, before I continue with this story, let me back up. You might be wondering, What exactly is Bio-Art, anyway?

*Bio-Art is an interdisciplinary field that merges art and biology. Artists in this space use living organisms, cells, or biotechnological tools to create work that explores themes of life, nature, and technology. It often raises ethical and philosophical questions about science, genetic engineering, and the way we interact with the natural world. Bio-Art can take many forms: lab-based experiments, installations, sculptures, and even performance art.*

Back to it then: The artists would dive into research, get stuck, and suddenly shift gears, go off in an entirely new direction, starting something seemingly unrelated. To the lab technicians, it seemed that the artists were playing, not taking lab time seriously. In reality, they were giving their subconscious minds the time to process, connect the dots, and find solutions. The artists knew that forcing it rarely leads to the best results. They trusted that if they gave their minds space, an answer would emerge, and that those playful detours would lead to unexpected breakthroughs. They did, time after time.

How does this relate to floral design? When I'm preparing for an event, I start "soft sketching in 3D." I play with materials, arrange and deconstruct them, flip them upside down, and see what happens. If something sparks my interest, I'll snap a photo or take a short video, then move on. Later, I might find my mind circling back to a particular shape or combination. It's a sign there's something worth exploring. This process is hard to describe because so much of it is intuitive, a learned instinct that develops over time. It's like that nagging feeling when you leave the house and wonder, "Did I leave the oven on?"

There's also something to be said about not forcing a solution. This idea aligns with the Eastern concept of wu-wei, which Alan Watts describes as "not forcing." I think of it as non-doing. It still requires action, but it happens naturally. Whenever I've rushed a solution, the result has felt (and honestly was) forced. Sure, I found a solution, but was it the best one? Hard to say. That's why I trust the process. Answers reveal themselves in time.

That's not to say deadlines and budgets don't matter. We live in the real world, and sometimes, you just have to make a call. But the more we refine this skill, the more efficient we become at knowing when to push and when to wait. This is why the saying "Art cannot be forced" holds weight. And yes, I realize this contradicts my whole "Do the Work" mantra from the first chapter, but hey, life is full of paradoxes. Don't be mistaken, gestation is doing the work. It's tapping into that quiet, inner intelligence. The key is staying mindful and making sure waiting doesn't slip into procrastination.

I like to think of it as a tiger, still and alert, waiting for just the right moment to pounce.

**Action:**

Finally, we get to some action, where the magic happens. After laying the groundwork and meticulously researching, it's time to bring ideas to life. I often tell new floral students that the actual design, the hands-on arranging, makes up only about 15-20% of the process. Sometimes, it feels even closer to 5%. This may be why some designers cling so tightly to the designing aspect; it's the most visibly creative part. However, impeccable execution, which is a much larger endeavor, requires structure, foresight, and practical know-how.

One of my first steps in any plan of action is preparing lists and sketches. Lists keep progress visible and provide that sweet satisfaction of checking off a task. Leading up to the execution of sample arrangements, I explore multiple centerpiece variations using insights from my initial walkthrough (or client conversation via phone or email), triggering that gestation period we discussed earlier. The goal is to refine the 'final' samples methodically, assembling them a day or two before the presentation. This will avoid the chaos of last-minute rushing caused by procrastination or perfectionism.

For site-specific floral installations, I start the day by gathering my team for a quick meeting. I outline the location, client expectations, and project objectives. I also present any sketches, 3D renderings, or visual guides. Just as crucial is setting intentions. In my experience, I've found that collaboration and shared creativity fuel the best outcomes far more than competition. Establishing clear intentions helps unify the team and keeps us aligned throughout the process.

While execution demands focus, it doesn't have to be devoid of playfulness. The best work happens in a balance of deep concentration and creative fluidity. This said, when I enter 'the zone,' I limit distractions. It's a sacred time of connection with something greater. If I see a team member in this state, I respect their process and ensure support without disruption. This is where having a well-structured studio and workflow becomes invaluable.

The euphoria of this flow state is what keeps us coming back. But as thrilling as it is to see an idea take form, this stage isn't without its challenges. Once we've begun, uncertainty, doubt, and unexpected hurdles often creep in. Transforming a vision into reality can be disorienting; what once appeared effortless in our minds now requires problem-solving and adaptability. This is where discomfort sets in, testing our resolve and pushing us to refine both our process and ourselves.

**Discomfort:**

Not soon after, we settle into this good feeling of, "Ah, this feels great; I've finally gotten started," we slowly transition into the next stage, where discomfort and/or boredom begin to take over. I don't know why this happens. I'm sure there is some psychological explanation for the processes that go deep into the workings of the mind when engaged in prolonged attentive-driven action, but I don't have the research. What I do know is that it is accurate. Perhaps it is similar to that voice in your mind when you run long distances.

This feeling is more prevalent the more exacting and tedious the piece you are engaged in. I also find this particularly prevalent in undisciplined florists/freelancers who begin working on centerpieces, for example, will get through three or four and then start looking for a distraction in the form of checking their phones, looking for coffee, or stopping altogether to tell a random story.  It is hard to watch and even more challenging to manage. This is mainly unconscious, so they do not realize they are in the transition of phases in the creative process. From experience, I know that giving in to this voice resets the whole process.

You could say, "What does it truly matter as long as you get back into it?" Okay, so let me be clear: if this is a case where a coping strategy is used to move past negative emotions, then this break and distraction may be warranted, as we will see a little later in the process. Of course, the world will not cease, and the job will eventually be done. However, if we can push through, we open ourselves to some of the most astounding aspects of the creative process: entering the zone state and experiencing the loss of the perspective of time.

If you've ever been engrossed in binge-watching a full season of a TV series in one day, well, you'll know what I'm talking about. What's better is you'll have something to show for it at the end. We've already touched on being in the zone and how magical it can be, and getting past the wall of boredom and frustration is one of the only ways in.

I constantly experience this loss of time in my studio, especially when I have a long list of activities for the day. It is like a vortex of time in there. This could also be related to not having a window in my space or another aspect of being in hyperfocus. Whatever the case, hours melt away in what feels like minutes.

In my experience, frustration is more common when dealing with new and unfamiliar tasks than simply feeling bored. At this stage in my career, cleaning flowers is something I can do without even thinking about it. So, the familiar feeling is boredom instead of frustration, and when I feel it arising, I begin switching focus and attention. Over the years, I have learned to make cleaning flowers a meditation practice: being in the moment of doing and watching the thoughts that arise and fall away as I work.

Frustration does show up during my creation process, but it is altogether different and is usually accompanied by negative self-talk. This generally comes up when working on something distinctly new or a project I am not necessarily jazzed about doing. How do you overcome it? Sometimes, it is enough to observe it, like a nagging child. Other times, if accompanied by negative emotions, I have found going into a state of gratitude helps. One recurring nagging thought is, "Why the hell am I wasting my time with this tiny project or task? I'm better than this." When this thought comes, it is good to remind myself that many people would love to have this job. This includes me! I also layer the idea with gratitude for having someone think of me to create this for them and pay me for it. I also layer these thoughts with imagining how much joy this will bring to the lives of the people who will view it.

Lastly, staying the course and pushing through these walls brings us to a high mental state of creativity where ideas flow more freely, challenges seem to solve themselves, and we're fully immersed in the work. This is the point where time disappears, and we don't leave feeling drained; we leave feeling invigorated, almost electrified. But, and this is a big but, that's only if we can get there.

Because sometimes, instead of hitting that creative flow, we slam into another, far less pleasant stage: the part where everything starts to look wrong. Doubt creeps in. That tiny voice in our head gets louder, insisting: This sucks!

## This Sucks!?

Why, you ask? Because usually, this is when discomfort turns into full-blown self-doubt, and that tiny voice in your head starts yelling at you, "This sucks!" Yep, this is a stage. It doesn't happen every time, but if you're creative, you've likely encountered this little *bastardo* at least once.

We'll dive deeper into negative self-talk in a later chapter, but for now, it's important to examine how it fits into the creative process. At this point, that nasty little voice in your head is doing everything it can to convince you that the best solution is to tear it all down and start over. And honestly, I've seen so many creatives do just that.

It's not hard to spot when someone has hit this phase. They start fidgeting, reworking their flowers, endlessly adjusting their mechanics, or even messing with their hair. It's as if their frustration needs a physical outlet. And if they aren't aware of what's happening, they'll often act on impulse and in a fit dismantle their work entirely.

Now, don't get me wrong, sometimes a fresh start *is* the best solution. But only if it comes from a place of clarity rather than frustration. A tantrum-driven reset, without a plan or direction, usually leads to the same outcome: another cycle of doubt and destruction.

So, what do you do when this happens? First, step away. Take a break, go for a short walk, grab a coffee, or even splash cold water on your face. A mental reset is crucial because it allows you to shift from an emotional reaction to an objective assessment. Once you've calmed your mind, ask yourself:

1) Is this truly a teardown project?
2) What was I originally looking to achieve?
3) What specifically is bothering me?
4) How can I pivot this idea into something interesting rather than starting from scratch?
5) If I did start over, what would I do differently?
6) Can I meet my original vision halfway from where I am now?
7) What would *[insert someone you admire]* do in this situation?
8) What are the simplest changes I can make to improve this piece?
9) Can I get a quick, reliable second opinion?

I ask my students these same questions when I see them getting stuck, and time after time, I watch the shift happen. Once you <u>demand</u> your mind to engage with problem-solving instead of panic, the solution often presents itself faster than you'd expect.

When I feel this way, I remind myself: "We are not throwing a tantrum right now. We are finding a solution and moving forward."

**Observation:**

At certain points in the creative process, especially in large-scale event work and installations, I need to step back and observe the project's direction. I do this several times, whether alone or with my team, but the key here is that observation is fluid; it isn't a rigid step but an ongoing practice.

For large-scale projects, stepping back is non-negotiable. It ensures that scale, proportion, and balance are maintained as the work evolves. But observation, in a larger sense, is pausing for a moment of reflection, not merely to check for symmetry or alignment, but to shift how you're seeing altogether. One of the techniques I teach in mural making is what I call "Soft Focus." You squint your eyes just enough to blur the details so the overall form comes into view. You're no longer seduced by the petals, the brush strokes, or textures; you're looking at shape, weight, and relationship. These days, I joke that I just have to take off my readers to achieve the same effect. But the point is this: **you must give yourself enough distance to see the whole.**

In my courses on large-scale installations, I let students work in teams, allowing them to navigate group dynamics and naturally assume roles. This mirrors how I run my freelance projects. Typically, students divide and conquer, breaking into smaller groups to tackle different sections of the installation. Sometimes, though, an individual seems adrift, either unsure of where to begin or hesitant to engage. When this happens, I pull them aside and assign them tasks that support the whole: prepping floral foam, cutting wire, or stripping leaves. These are small but essential components of production. And interestingly, these students often end up learning the most.

At around the two-thirds mark of an installation, I call for a hard stop. Everyone steps back, and we do a quiet observation. For a full minute, we say nothing. This means no adjustments, no movement, just looking. Then, I ask the group two simple questions:

- What is this?
- What still needs to be done?

The extroverts usually rush to answer, and I often have to redirect them to keep it concise. The goal isn't a drawn-out critique at that point, but a brief, objective assessment of the work in its current state. Then, we return to silence to absorb the work again. This moment is crucial. It teaches students the power of stepping back without reacting, something that isn't emphasized enough in traditional education.

This moment of collective silence, when we step back and simply SEE, often reveals more than any critique. It's where clarity begins to take shape, which, for me, always demands commitment.

**If you're going to make a move, make it all the way.**

This is something I've learned again and again, both in the studio and on the job site: If a design choice feels timid or halfway done, it reads that way. Ideas die in hesitation. When you go in full force, with intention, even if imperfect, you give the audience something to trust. Something to hold onto. Confusion comes when we second-guess or soften the impact to play it safe.

From this point, I shift into creative director mode, giving each group a refined task list: priorities to unify the piece, corrections to ensure cohesion, and final adjustments to make the installation feel like one complete work rather than a patchwork of ideas. I do this in front of the whole class, not to single anyone out, but to establish collective accountability. The message is clear: to bring the vision together, the work must read as one cohesive piece.

I also use silent, objective observation in my fine art practice. At the end of each studio session, I document my progress, reviewing what's been done and what needs attention next. This sober, deliberate assessment is just as crucial in solo work as it is in collaborative projects.

**Action...Or More Research:**

After completing the initial stages, we usually progress with ongoing actions. However, this action isn't always a straightforward next step; it may require revisiting our work with additional research or conducting further experiments.

This is one of the curious yet inevitable stages in the process, where continued action is intertwined with further research. It's an ongoing cycle where you take action, step back, and then dive deeper into the creative process, almost in erratic mini-cycles. You might find yourself revisiting ideas, revising your approach, or experimenting with different materials, sometimes more than once, before landing on the final result.

After a period of silent observation, when I feel ready to re-enter the work, it often comes with renewed clarity and a sense of direction. Revisiting previous steps in the creative process is an essential part of refinement. Embrace the ebb and flow of it. Be open to experimentation and trust that these mini-cycles, even if they feel disruptive at times, lead to creative breakthroughs. It's all part of it.

**Finished:**

So, when is a piece truly finished? It's tough to say, especially with painting and sculpture. Ask me about how I found out how tough it can actually be in closing out this book! We have to "feel it." Yes, this might sound like a non-answer, but it's the best one I've got. In floral design, it's a bit easier when the flowers are used up and time runs out; that's when it's done. I often joke with students: When the client says, "Oh my god, this arrangement is gorgeous!" that's your cue, drop your tools and wrap it up! Anything beyond that, and you're just fussing with the flowers.

This can be a tough truth for newer designers, and trust me, I've been there. I think it's because they haven't created enough arrangements yet to feel confident about when to stop. In my early days as a junior florist, I wanted every arrangement to be perfect every time. I was determined to do as much as I could with each design, to make every moment last. The reality? I was bruising and damaging the flowers the longer I overworked them.

I'll never forget what my old boss and original teacher would say: "Juan, that's enough. It's beautiful! You're falling in love with it! Get it out the door!" Hilarious and accurate, and I still carry those words of wisdom with me today.

Art, though, is more complicated. Finishing a piece might mean simply packing it away in storage, whether or not it was successful. I've created plenty of pieces that didn't turn out as planned, but I see them as learning opportunities. Eventually, I have to call it done and move on. As

I've matured, I've found that I don't throw out 'unsuccessful' art as much as I used to. All the work I create serves as a snapshot or a moment in time, and it holds the potential for reinterpretation down the road.

While this isn't quite the same in my floral or gardening work, where fulfilling the contract and shipping the work is often the final step, I do see a similarity. Whether the piece is "good" or "bad," we learn, we move on, and we keep practicing.

**Analysis:**

This brings us to the next part of the process: analysis. Analysis is crucial in shaping how we view our work and, ultimately, how we improve. I make it a point to meet with my team after particularly large or complex installations to review what we've created. Critique is an essential part of this process...and it should never be taken personally.

Over the years, I've learned how to frame critiques more effectively, focusing on both the successes and the areas for improvement. I've also incorporated this into my classes, and the students have generally responded positively. The key here is not to make critique feel like a negative experience. I anchor the process with a simple phrase: *"Ya para la próxima"* or "For next time."

There's a method of critiquing where you sandwich positive and negative statements. I do use this approach sometimes, but I prefer to be honest rather than adhering strictly to a formulaic critique. In my experience, there's always something positive to say about every piece, and I usually find something compelling that speaks to me. I focus the discussion on these aspects first. Sometimes, even if the overall piece isn't a total success, there may be a moment of intrigue, a seed of inspiration, or a question it raises that calls for further exploration. In my opinion, that's a huge win.

An important part of any critique, especially when working with students or emerging artists, is ensuring they understand that I see the potential in their work. My goal is never to criticize them but to help them meet their own expectations and encourage their growth. As a coach, teacher, and mentor, my role is to facilitate the birth of their ideas, helping them refine and evolve. This isn't about being a scolding authority figure, but rather being a supportive partner in their journey.

Here are some of the questions I ask myself and my team when reviewing a completed piece, in no particular order:

1) How is the overall movement, color composition, and choice of materials?

2) Did we stay on budget, or did I overbuy unnecessary floral products?

3) Are we happy with what we produced? Does it elicit a visceral response from the viewer?

4) Could we have used a more efficient method of setup?

5) Did our mechanics hold up, or did we overdo them unnecessarily?

6) Does the design function as intended?

7) What feedback have we received from viewers and the client?

8) Did we cooperate and communicate efficiently and respectfully as a team?

9) Are we all exhausted and overworked, or do we feel like we've been in a brawl? This feeling sometimes creeps up, and it's worth acknowledging.

10) Did we meet our initial set of intentions?

I want to emphasize the importance of taking the time to reflect on your completed projects and learn from them. I've seen designers, even some highly successful ones, who rush through entire seasons, jumping from event to event without ever pausing to assess and analyze their work. As a result, they make the same mistakes over and over, leading to exhausted teams, resentful crew members, and chaotic profit margins. Stack those kinds of seasons together, and before long, you may find yourself shutting your doors, with your vendors chasing after you.

**What's Next:**

In this final section, I call "What's Next?" At this stage, we prepare ourselves to begin the process anew. Specifically, I'm referring to the moments after a large event when the adrenaline has faded, and it's time to reflect on the breakdown. I take the opportunity to do a quick inventory before storing everything back in our loft. I check what supplies need to be refilled and assess what can wait for later. I also make sure our default tool bags are reorganized and ready for the next installation.

Ideally, I'll already have another project in the prep or research phase, or at least one in the works. Stacking projects or events when possible is part of my practice protocol; it keeps the momentum flowing and ensures there's always something on the horizon. We'll dive deeper into this strategy in a future chapter because it plays a vital role in maintaining a healthy creative psyche.

One last note: as the initial diagram shows, we may skip over certain parts of the process. Despite having a structured system in place, I believe it's crucial to leave space for spontaneity. The real secret to understanding the creative process is having a roadmap that allows for flexibility and growth. This framework has been invaluable throughout my career, especially during times when I feel adrift in a sea of emotions and self-doubt. It serves as an anchor, helping me hold true, surrender, and trust the process.

## Reflections:

– What section of the Creative Process do you resonate with the most?

– Where do you feel most lost or most at home?

– Is "trust the process" helpful for you, or does it feel like empty advice?

# PART II:

## FORMATION

The forging process of internal growth that develops the integrity and character in the work.

# 6

# PATIENCE

It started almost as a joke, me taping down a sheet of watercolor paper on my Ikea butcher block worktable. That paper was found buried in a stack of old art supplies, and I figured it might be helpful. A practical place to jot down seasonal to-dos or inventory. I told myself I'd just white out and reuse the list as needed.

But that simple gesture opened a door I didn't expect.

Before long, interns and freelancers circled the table, unsure whether they could prep flowers or set vases on it. "Cover it with cellophane if it bugs you," I'd tell them. But somewhere along the way, the paper started to feel like art. Eventually, I peeled it off the table and added a few final touches.

That's when I realized I'd also been circling the subject for far too long. Making excuses after excuses for why I couldn't make art.

So, I scaled up. I stapled a large canvas to the floor of my studio. Same idea. "Think of it like a rug," I told my team. "Don't worry about it." I wasn't worried either. I was too absorbed to. I was still running events, juggling clients, and managing my gardening practice. But now, art was creeping back in. Sometimes, as an additional intentional scuff or an all-too-obvious dripping of extra paint on that floor canvas.

Those small gestures started to accumulate, stirring in me something I had been suppressing. This came even as the business appeared to be peaking on paper, and signs of burnout were slowly increasing. I kept thinking, "It's time for a change."

I even applied to a high-profile artist residency, which seems almost laughable in hindsight. But I was serious, taking another big shot, not limiting what is possible for my life. My wife looked at me sideways:
"Why would you want to do that?"
"How would that even fit into your schedule?"

Fair questions. But I didn't overthink it. I just knew I needed to see what my work looked like again, because I no longer recognized it. I also knew wholeheartedly that the art world didn't fully take floral design seriously. At least not then, not really. I wanted to be taken seriously. By them. But more importantly, by myself.

I started making. Testing rusty hands. Playing with materials and ideas. Nothing was off limits. But internally, the pressure was mounting. I developed brutal neck pain, and when I went to the doctor, he found nothing wrong.

"You might want to talk to a therapist," he said.

"A therapist, really, Ok," I replied, so as not to sound defensive.

What I was really thinking was: "You think I'm losing it, don't you?"

We'll come back to that because life had other plans. But spoiler alert: he was right, therapy changed everything.

Then the pandemic hit. The studio went quiet. The halls of my studio building were now empty, doors locked. No clients. No coworkers. No casual drop-ins. Just me and the silence. Stickers outside my door, marking every six feet. Inside the floor canvas I'd been stepping over suddenly became the art itself. I wasn't sure what I was chasing anymore, but I knew I had to keep moving my hands, even if only for myself.

I finally had something I hadn't had in years: time. Time to sit. To listen. To watch the work. The gestures became bolder, sometimes subtle, sometimes violent, but steady. I made the most out of whatever was around. Eventually, I had real work again. A portfolio I could stand behind.

Now the studio <u>had to</u> share space with the art, while still tending to the essential gardening business. Because it had finally fully returned, or maybe I had returned to it.

But with that came a new question: "How do I explain this?"

As the team began trickling back in, I found myself looking for ways to justify the shift. "What was this stuff?" "How did it connect to flowers, to the plants, to the work we were doing every day?" For years, I'd treated my art school background like a footnote. I was a florist. A gardener. Only a few people still called me "artist," the folks back home, and a handful of friends from Chicago.

Now the lines were starting to blur.

I started gifting pieces to clients. I started saying the word "artist" out loud even though it felt risky. It felt like fallout. Like I'd skipped the sports car and gone for acrylic paints and plaster instead.

I'd never said it before, "artist and florist" in the same breath, not in public, because I worried it would muddy the waters. And to be fair, at first, it did. But at that point, I felt stripped down, bare.

What more could I lose?

Eventually, I got a residency. A solo show. And as has somehow always been true in my life, the art started to sell again. Slowly. Painfully slowly. But it moved.

In hindsight, I see now that the thread running through all of this was patience.

**Cultivation of patience:**

Learning to recognize the season we're in can be one of the most powerful tools a creative person possesses. Are we in a planting season? A growing one? A time of harvest? Or a stretch of stillness, when the field lies fallow where the work happens beneath the surface?

Each phase carries its own needs, and within each, we also learn how to measure our progress with compassion.

Sit with that for a moment because we cannot rush the seasons. This is the development of presence in the process.

Yes, we've already talked about picking up skills on the creative path. But this one, Patience, is something deeper. It's a core component of the life we have been talking about building.

At every turn, our patience is tested, and in turn, it must be practiced.

Looking back now, I realize that artistic break I took while building my business may have been a kind of emotional insulation. Maybe I knew, even then, that the floral business would take root faster than the long, often slow work of artistic development. And coming back into it, I have such a wealth of insights that I never would have had if I had only continued on the trajectory I was on, without letting the soil breathe.

Only this time, I've laid down the hourglass on my creative practice.

I used to treat art with a stopwatch. "I've got to rush and finish this piece up because I have until 5 pm before I have to switch gears to write the estimate for that upcoming event." Now, I let the work breathe. I know it'll be there when I return. A successful art career by 50, 60, or 70; these are imaginary deadlines. They don't advance the work.

My creative life now runs on care for my body, for my mind, for the pace I can reasonably keep. I remind myself often: going slow is not failure. There is no finish line, no stopwatch. Only forward motion. However small.

Developing more patience in putting off tasks when rest is required has also taken time. I'm finding this especially true now; in the writing of this book, we are getting back into full swing post-pandemic. At least here in New York City, it seems people are rushing around faster than ever, seemingly to compensate for the lost time. Amidst this, I've made a conscious effort to ease back into the rat race more slowly. I've prioritized my mental health and developed a broader, more ART-inclusive work ethic that allows for a slower pace as my work progresses. I am committed to these habits to avoid falling back into old patterns and losing the rich ground I've nurtured. I have come to realize that if I take time off for self-care, the world will not collapse; it will continue, and so will I.

**Finding Grace and Understanding:**

Yes, I know some people's careers in the creative arts take off like rockets, but this is not my story. I have had to work hard and persistently to accomplish what I have. Some days, I think, "I still know nothing!" because even modest achievements can seem like climbing sandy mountains in my low moments and during challenging times.

Even so, my mother's consistent response to almost all of my even modest achievements is, "Gosh darn it, you are so talented, *hijo*! I could never do that," which has admittedly seemed like dismissive pleasantries from my doting mother. I often felt the struggle to communicate my feelings to her, as her compliments always seemed to overlook and skirt the painstaking effort behind my perceived minuscule progress. Or, I'd negate the work by saying, "Oh, it's a team effort." However, I now understand how this reflected my insecurities rather than her heartfelt, honest intentions.

When those emotions surfaced, I overlooked her perspective, one shaped by her own distinct experiences and the challenges she's faced as a single Latina mother and entrepreneur. Her compliments, through that lens, were sincere expressions of love, pride, and admiration.

I've come to see how my own emotions and insecurities have shaped the way I receive praise. For a long time, I struggled to let compliments in. I'd deflect or downplay them, sometimes without even realizing it. Not because I didn't value the words, but because part of me didn't feel entirely worthy of them.

It's taken time, a lot of time, to realize how deeply that pattern runs, how easily self-doubt can distort even the kindest sentiments. Learning to pause, to let the words land without resistance, has become part of the work of instilling patience into the practice. A grounded kind of healing.

As a mental health practice, I'm cultivating patience with myself, particularly when my artistic career seems to progress slowly. I'm learning to recognize compliments for their genuine intent instead of distorting them through my own perceptions. All this serves as a reminder that patience, self-awareness, and understanding play crucial roles in overcoming self-doubt. Ultimately, everything unfolds in its own time, and time indeed proves to be a great healer, as the saying goes.

**A Moment for Rest:**

Dormancy is vital to all life forms. In plants, it happens in both the seasons and the daily cycles of light and dark. Growth happens in waves, in rest and renewal. In the slow seasons of our careers, the winters aren't wasted time. They're periods of gestation, of gathering strength.

Even when we think we've mapped out our place in the cycle, life has a way of surprising us. Setbacks, delays, droughts, and floods can wreak havoc on our neatly ordered plans. For my younger readers, I know you've come of age in an era where disruption isn't the exception. It can feel like nothing is stable, nothing predictable. But this, too, is a phase, and like everything else, it will shift. Flowers don't bloom just because we want them to. Slumps don't lift on schedule. Instead, the work and the clarity come in their own appointed time.

In a world plugged in and wired for hustle, it's easy to forget this. We've all seen the mantras: "Let them sleep while I grind." And honestly, that phrase makes me cringe. Over the years, I've learned that nurturing a healthy, balanced mindset is a more gentle and intelligent approach. Pushing past the point of exhaustion, physically or creatively, rarely yields anything worth keeping.

I discovered this early through marathon sleepovers with my cousin. We slowly realized the futility of pushing ourselves beyond exhaustion.

Even back then, it was clear: no matter how much we wanted to 'win' against sleep, our bodies always had their own agenda.

Back then, we thought we were invincible, hopped up on sugar, soda, carbs, and a hefty dose of ego, chasing some vague trophy of endurance. Honestly, we were like the kids from every wild sleepover movie ever made. We'd swear we were going to stay awake for 24 hours. We'd make a night of it to prove we could. We took turns playing video games, one of us resting while the other kept vigil. As the night dragged on, our eyes would sting, our heads would ache, and we'd reluctantly migrate to the couch, watching TV in the dark. That's when the irritability set in, bickering over who was about to fall asleep first, then reconvincing each other to keep going. Inevitably, the caffeine would catch up with us, and one of us would have to break for the bathroom. That's when the Sandman would strike. We'd come back to find the other knocked out, no matter how disciplined we thought we were.

I don't remember if we ever made it to 24 hours. It wasn't until later that we realized how bad that kind of sleep deprivation was for our young bodies and minds. We're not built to function without rest. We need periods of stillness biologically, creatively, and emotionally.

And if there's one big takeaway from this, it's that real momentum and longevity come from knowing when to pause, not constant motion.

**Letting Go of Comparison:**

It has taken a great deal of presence of mind to allow myself to breathe, make mistakes, pivot when needed, and set realistic expectations for where I am at any given moment. Extending that same grace to myself and, frankly, to others in my world has been one of the biggest lessons I've slowly learned as I've matured as a creative. A lot of that has to do with accepting the realities of my physical, fiscal, and mental limits.

While we're in this frame of mind, it feels like the right moment to revisit a topic from an earlier chapter. There, I talked about the importance of seeking help from professionals and letting go of the shame that can come with asking for it. And while it might seem like a detour here, stay with me.

If you remember, I shared some regret about wearing too many hats early on, like the time I tried to handle a photo shoot for my business website myself because, frankly, I couldn't afford to hire anyone. It wasn't so much about the pride. I honestly just didn't have the money. I knew it would have been better to get professional help, and I watched peers do it without hesitation, but it just wasn't an option for me at the time. The harsh reality is that sometimes the best option available to you remains a shitty one, and that's part of how we learn life's lessons along the way.

That experience ultimately taught me new skills and even sparked new passions. I picked up photography out of necessity, and what started as a workaround became something I genuinely enjoyed. Looking back in this way, I can frame it as a positive turning point, not a failure. It taught me patience, resourcefulness, and the importance of setting expectations based on what's possible in the moment, not on what others are doing.

The reality is, growing a business or creative practice takes time, resources, and a lot of flexibility. And those resources aren't the same for everyone. When I was building my website, sure, I probably could have made some big sacrifices to pay for a photographer. But I wasn't ready for that, mentally or financially. So instead, I leaned into what I had, tapped into my creative problem-solving, and made it work. This lesson taught me about photography, balance, timing, and knowing when to ask for help. Above all, it taught me to recognize when it makes sense for me.

**Progress On My Own Terms:**

As we evaluate our lives, it's important to consider that we are spiritual beings with limitless potential, and our current circumstances don't define our true essence. When we reflect, it's important to focus on our own progress, without measuring it against someone else's timeline.

Even the Ten Commandments caution against envying what others possess. Throughout history, many speakers have reiterated this idea in various forms...but the core message remains unchanged. Remember, no one else is living our lives; while there may be shared experiences, each of us has our unique narrative, and self-evaluation should be based on our distinct realities.

Letting go slowly, intentionally, of the need to measure my success against others has created a massive paradigm shift in how I see my work and my place in it. It hasn't been instant, but it's reshaped the way I move through my career and how I measure progress on my terms. That change didn't happen out of nowhere. It was a result of loss and the necessity to keep going despite it, and that, in turn, made it a more challenging issue to confront.

**Behind a Smile:**

Tapping into this awareness, I'm reminded of what a former mentor once told me, "You never know what is happening in someone else's world." It sounded simple at the time, but those words have stayed with me. We're all experts at holding it together, at maintaining facades out of fear of judgment or simply survival. It's hard enough to be honest with ourselves some days, let alone convey our intentions or struggles to anyone else.

That truth hit differently during one of the hardest stretches of my life, a time I referenced earlier when I joked about a doctor recommending therapy, and I brushed it off. "We'll come back to that because life had other plans," I said. Well, this was it.

In the space of a few years, I experienced a string of losses: my floral delivery driver, my mother-in-law, and my dog, all gone unexpectedly. At the same time, I was running my business, managing events, and showing up every day as if nothing had changed. I wore a cheerful face because people depended on me. I didn't want to disappoint them or be a bummer. But inside, I was unraveling. I buried myself in work. I convinced myself I was coping when, in truth, I was avoiding. The grief didn't just stay in my head; it settled firmly into my body. The neck pain I'd brushed off months earlier turned out to be a physical manifestation of everything I hadn't allowed myself to feel or process. And when I finally started to work through that grief, the pain disappeared.

The magnitude of loss has been staggering in the wake of the pandemic, especially here in New York City. I often wonder how many thousands are navigating the same vulnerable state I found myself in during those dark days. I remember feeling that I was just one insult or compliment away from breaking down in tears. Looking back, struggling unknowingly with emotional exhaustion made everything so much more challenging. The memory of this fragile state of mind reminds me to be patient with people and, more importantly, myself.

I've made it a practice to remind myself that I will never have the whole story, nor can I ever truly know the extent of someone's pain, often hidden behind an obligatory smile. If you find yourself in a similar season of your life, I encourage you to reach out for help and find someone to talk to. I did, and it transformed my life, allowing me to heal.

My doctor was right. Therapy didn't just help, it changed everything. It gave me language for what I'd been carrying. It helped me see how art, business, grief, and identity were all tangled together. And it reminded me that everyone we encounter is carrying an invisible truth: You never know what's behind a smile.

**Ok, But How Long Will This All Take?:**

Being mindful of our journeys and those of others around us requires patience, indeed. And what I end up swirling back to in thinking of this is this issue of comparison and navigating self-imposed timelines. Which brings me to the questions I hear all the time from students:

"So, how long should it take before I land my first storefront? Or consistent wedding bookings? Or regular corporate accounts?"

The short, vague answer: "It depends."

But seriously, to answer that question meaningfully, you have to circle back to all the issues we've already unpacked. So when people ask me, I often counter with: Compared to what? Compared to whom? Because time is relative. And in this Insta-fed world we all inhabit, it's easy to underestimate how long it actually takes to see traction, for the tides to shift, or for people to even know you exist.

In conversations with my mom, this theme has come up countless times. She always says it takes at least five to eight years to establish a business, to settle in, be found by customers, and build consistency. "*Pero, hijo,* the most important thing is they get your phone number," she always reminds me with a laugh. And honestly, she's not wrong.

For younger readers, maybe swap "phone number" for your e-shop link, your DMs, your booking portal, whatever makes your work reachable and reliable.

Those same benchmarks still hold up, at least in my experience. It took those years for my business to gain traction in New York's highly competitive market. I did it by stacking small wins, delivering the work, documenting it, and following up on leads. Over time, those small jobs and quiet wins taught me how to be ready.

**When You're Ready:**

I've had to develop immense patience in building my event business. Every single stage mattered from learning basic bookkeeping at my mother's kitchen table, to freelancing large-scale galas in Manhattan, to figuring out how to balance client demands without losing myself in the process.

So when people ask, "How long will it take?"

The blunt, compassionate answer is: "When you're ready."

This truth also applies to personal growth and the practical realities of running a business. Looking back, I realize I often yearned for opportunities even when I wasn't completely ready. The spiritual aspect of this suggests that readiness comes with the experience, not just desire alone. Had I achieved my dream of a solo studio earlier, I would have struggled with the realities of running a professional workspace. The waiting, the challenges, and the setbacks all served a purpose, making the final achievement that much more rewarding.

**Find a Good Stopping Point:**

Another lesson that's stayed with me came from my high school art teacher, Mrs. Canales. She wasn't like anyone else I knew growing up. That Scandinavian woman in my small hometown thought differently. She encouraged me to lean into Mexican art history, to claim visual languages I didn't yet understand had a place in a larger canon. I realize now what a gift it was to get that push to imagine myself inside a lineage when I barely knew what one was.

That mural, which Mrs. Canales had our high school commission me to paint outside the library atrium, was still there a few years ago. I stopped by, hoping to document it before the school remodeled. To my surprise, it wasn't rough around the edges or hokie or even sun-faded as I imagined it might be. It still felt like my work.

She used to tell us, as the bell neared, to "Find a good stopping point" so we could pick up easily the next day. I've carried that with me through every chapter of my career in writing, artmaking, and business. Knowing when to pause is as important as knowing when to push. It's one of the reasons I didn't collapse completely during those brutal years of loss and burnout. It gave me permission to leave things unfinished, to return later, to pace myself.

I can't help but smile when my wife lovingly teases me about my patience or, more accurately, my lack of it. I will concede, I'm always working on it. I often hear life coaches say, "Success isn't a destination, it's about who we become during the journey." That sentiment resonates deeply with me.

Looking back, I see how patience has shaped me as an artist, a business owner, and a person. Maybe it's age, or experience, or perhaps it's all those unpretentious, easily overlooked moments, like when I taped a piece of watercolor paper to my butcher block table, that have quietly ignited the turning points. It could also be how all of it has come together, each moment one separate but essential piece of a much larger puzzle.

Whatever the case, I've come to accept that patience isn't mastered overnight. It develops naturally, but only if you make the effort to nurture it. Patience is indeed a virtue, but it is also a practice within your practice, one that strengthens with continuous use.

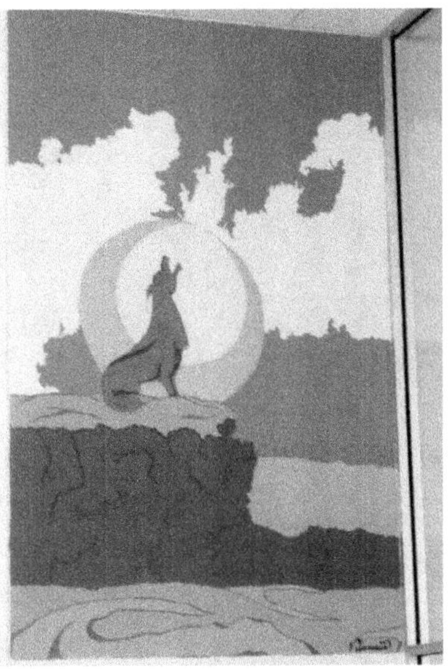

This Coyote Mural at Alice High School, commissioned following Mrs. Canales' recommendation. Photo by me.

# Reflections:

– How have you struggled with patience? How did you come through it?

– Has surrendering to patience ever healed something in you?

– Where do you believe patience comes from: time, effort, experience, or something else?

# 7

# ON LEADERSHIP

It was a small installation, not even real floral work. Just styling. Potted tulips in tiny galvanized tins for the hightops, a custom-painted portable chalkboard mural, a balloon arch, and balloon florals assembled and meant to look like spring in Central Park. But something in me clicked that day: I treated it like a flagship. I showed up with printed freelancer contracts, day-of agendas, and new crew hoodies labeled by size and packed with care. Absolutely, it was overkill. But it was a moment when I knew:

"This is mine. And I want to do this right."

I think about that version of me now; so full of intention, structure, clarity. Mimicking the ultra-luxury event companies I had been working for. And I don't judge myself too harshly...I needed that disciplined approach. I was building trust with myself first.

But leadership shifts, especially as the work scales. And what begins with overly curated care can mutate under pressure, due to the imposing weight of responsibility, shifting into fear, into control.

Years later, I found myself on my hands and knees at the Javits, soaking up soiled water with scraps of paper I had dug out of the recycling bins minutes before the show opened.

Alongside all the 'usual' florals, for that production, we had built four massive floral gardens, each measuring eight feet tall, sixteen feet wide, and six feet deep. The team had gone above and beyond. We were dead tired. And then, right before the doors opened, someone spilled a full bucket of dirty water across the clean entrance carpet we had been guarding for three days.

She froze, her face gone white.

All that 'patience' I just harped on about in the last chapter, I lost all of it.

I snapped. "Keep moving! Find something to soak it up!" I barked. I crouched, hands raw, dabbing as quickly as possible to save what I could.

I pleaded to the crew, "GET HELP! FIND THE CUSTODIANS! We are not allowed to use the mops ourselves here!"

My chest was pounding. I don't remember breathing; the sound went out muffled like I was underwater. The only sound was in my head, a recording of the countless repeated conversations I had leading up to the installation, that went, "Please watch out for the carpeting...It's a pain point for the executives."

It wasn't my best moment. Not because I was wrong to demand a quick response. But because I was carrying it all alone. I lost my resolve and broke trust with my crew.

I thought the work was <u>all mine to protect</u>. But it never was. And in chasing perfection, I missed a chance to lead with grace.

That day, something cracked open in me. I had to face the bullheaded ownership of "this is mine, and mine alone." Slowly, I've started to let go, realizing this is instead OUR work, mine, the crew's, and the clients'. I started realizing that leading means making space for people to carry it with you. That we grow not by gripping tighter, but by loosening our grip and trusting the wind to carry what's ready to go.

Leadership, at its core, is not a crown you wear. It's a garden you tend. And sometimes, it's mostly filled with dandelions you watch over briefly before the wind takes hold, and all you're left to do is allow the seeds to spread and to become something else entirely.

That moment at the Javits marked a turning point in how I understood professionalism and leadership. Allowing space for mistakes and working hard to provide a supportive environment that also allows space for embracing imperfection and growth.

**Leadership in the Creative Fields:**

Leadership sneaks up on you. It creeps into our lives as we begin managing ourselves. One day, you're just working to keep the movement flowing, and the next, people are looking to you for direction, clarity, and confidence you may not always feel. This chapter arrives alongside Patience for good reason; the two are rarely separated in real-world practice. Where patience steadies us, leadership moves us forward. The two are typically working in tandem.

In creative fields such as floristry, leadership often differs from what we might automatically think of. In the arts, I see it more as managing project uncertainties and guiding my team through chaos, rather than solely making decisions or assigning tasks, though those are still important. This type of leadership training isn't commonly offered in many art or floral programs. Usually, leadership in the floral industry is discussed only in terms of managing staffing or logistics. However, I've realized over time that leadership is an equally important artistic skill. It influences how we execute high-stakes installations, support each other during tense moments, and remain committed to the broader vision, even under pressure.

In the pages that follow, I'll share some of the challenges I've faced, the lessons that stuck, and the small but powerful ways creative leadership shows up on the job.

**The Inner Work:**

At every stage, the toughest person I had to lead... was myself. I had to learn how to address my inadequacies consistently. It's been humbling. These shortcomings often manifest as feeling like I have something to prove, struggling with feelings of not being enough, people-pleasing(a huge one for me), and grappling with a sense of unworthiness. Working through these challenges has allowed me to feel more secure in letting go, listening to my team, adapting, relaxing, and moving forward confidently with big projects. By addressing my flaws and calming my troubled mind, I've made it easier to avoid making complicated matters more difficult than necessary.

When I first started my business, I put so much unnecessary pressure on myself to build an impeccable brand. This doesn't mean I've discarded all of my standards. Rather, it means I've learned to accept certain inherent truths about large-scale production and adjust as needed. Remembering, first and foremost, that we cannot lead if there is no one to lead. Maintaining a healthy community mindset has become a key part of that process.

**A Shift in Perspective:**

It's crucial to recognize from the outset that the principles we've talked about extend beyond theory. They hold practical relevance in our daily professional interactions. Leaders need to exercise patience regularly with clients, peers, and their teams. Yet, I've noticed something curious not just in floristry, but also in other service-based industries. People often treat clients like adversaries, rather than partners.

I've seen it happen in countless studios, workshops, and schools. Designers vent frustration about demanding clients, only to be the same people who complain when business slows down. It's a paradox that reveals a more profound truth: our mindset around leadership and relationships directly affects our success. I say this based on my own personal experiences that I've had to put into check, often.

As leaders, we must acknowledge that conflict is an inevitable part of human interactions. But it's how we handle these conflicts that defines us. As leaders, we're called to examine how we feel about a situation and why. When resentment creeps in, it's often a sign that friction has entered, and this may stem from a misalignment that can be cultural, procedural, or even personal.

Make no mistake, client relationships are still relationships, and just like personal ones, they can become toxic. When resentment and negativity begin to seep into our interactions, it affects not just one project but our entire creative practice. Knowing when to step back, reframe, or even walk away is a leadership skill in itself.

**With Clients:**

To shift perspective in conflict, I consciously look at the situation from a different angle. One example I often face is in waiting for clients to respond to estimates or payments. But clients generally aren't late with a response because they're disrespectful. Life happens. Leadership means holding firm timelines and flexible empathy. I've had to learn when to nudge, when to wait, and when to walk. Each of these decisions is made on a case-by-case basis. There could be many reasons for the delay, and it's not necessarily because they're intentionally avoiding you, wasting your time, or going elsewhere to undercut an estimate.

We all encounter the unexpected, and recognizing this can keep us from jumping to conclusions. A victim mentality, often rooted in past experiences or unresolved trauma, can distort our perception of situations and people. I came to understand this more clearly through years of therapy. Maintaining healthy relationships requires patience and the humility to accept that life doesn't always move at our pace. When we take the time to identify and work through these deeper patterns, we can respond with greater empathy, clarity, and strength.

**With Vendors:**

These principles also apply to relationships with vendors. My vendors are some of the best in the industry and are stand-up individuals. That said, errors occasionally occur with our orders, whether it's flowers that get held up in customs, arrive dead, or come in the wrong color, or planters that arrive broken or in the wrong size. It's Murphy's Law at work.

When these situations arise, I have a choice: I could confront the vendor angrily, or I could pivot quickly and focus on finding a sound solution. Decisions made in the heat of the moment, when I'm all up in my feelings, have never been good ones.

Instead, what I do now is take a breather, recenter myself, quickly go into solution mode, and worry about the blame game, honestly.... NEVER. Placing blame never benefits anyone and is a massive waste of time and energy. From personal experience, it takes a cool head, especially when thousands of dollars and our reputation are on the line. Trusting in our vendors means knowing they're not intentionally sabotaging our order. In fact, they are most likely just as invested in getting it right as you are. The issue is nearly never personal; it's simply part of the complexity of the work we do.

Being strategic with vendor relationships in general is a mature leadership mindset. If my response is always reactive, I close up the channels of communication where early warnings live. Leaders at their best cultivate trust. When problems arise, they can be addressed early, fostering accountability and open communication. The creative industries are complex enough, and we all face immense pressure, especially during the event seasons. As leaders, it is our responsibility to control our emotions and have patience with one another.

**With Co-Workers:**

As mentioned, I typically hire freelance subcontractors to help with larger installations, especially during the event season. During this time, it's easy for individuals to become overbooked as we all strive to maximize our billable hours within the short seasons. Additionally, it's important to remind myself that the people I employ have families and other personal commitments. This requires patience, respect, and an understanding that everyone has a life outside of work.

Once again, this comes back to open communication. In my years in the industry, I've found that you can lead by fear; this may motivate people temporarily, but it will never earn true respect. On the other hand, when you lead with respectful, empowering dialogue, people feel comfortable sharing what's going on in their lives and will work with you. They're more likely to let you know ahead of time if they can't meet a commitment or expectation.

The driving force behind this is intention. Leaders have the patience to understand that investing time in their people will eventually create more leaders within the company. A boss, on the other hand, is short-sighted and demands results immediately, without consideration. Leaders demonstrate their values through their actions, and a boss demands (no questions asked).

**The Leap:**

When I took the leap of faith and started my company, I didn't have investors, a polished business plan, or even a safety net. What I had in commitment was a few clients who said, "We'll call you when we need work." This, along with a haunting sense that I couldn't keep waiting for someone else to hand me permission. The flower shop I worked at was already showing signs that it was slowly failing, and those early clients saw the writing on the wall, too. So when I finally left, and the shop closed, they started to trickle in.

In full disclosure, my first business deposit was only a few thousand dollars, everything I had to my name. There was no room for failure. I started with simple weekly accounts from the corner of my living room, reinvesting every dollar outside my rent into the business. It was an exciting, exhilarating, and scary time. The hardest part was overcoming the fear of "Where will my next paycheck come from?" In my regular jobs, I was used to knowing exactly when and how much I'd get paid. Now, that was all up in the air, and the fear of uncertainty was almost too much to bear. I nearly didn't take the initial leap and even applied to several high-end flower shops as a backup. Looking back, I realize how lucky I was that none of those shops hired me. Those rejections gave me the push I needed.

**Slow Growth Builds Strong Roots:**

Around the time I had created the tulips in tin's job, one of my favorite vendors asked me how my business was doing, noting that he had seen me around more frequently. I told him I had recently moved into a studio just down the street, but I also mentioned that I'd been building my business at a steady pace. He nodded thoughtfully and said, "You know, Juan, this is the best way. When you build slowly, you make smaller mistakes and learn more along the way. That makes for a stronger company in the long run. People come in here, spend a year or two buying everything, and then, after a couple of years, you never see them again. They don't know how to manage a business that explodes in size without the experience."

Those are wise words and ones I've come to appreciate deeply. Nothing can truly prepare you for the meteoric rise of a career, no matter how much book smarts or talent you may have. That said, I've also seen businesses that defy this trend. It's rare, but in those cases, it seems like there's an impeccable network of business managers, solid financial backing, and a disciplined team running the operation.

Alas, that's not my story.

**The Freelancer:**

To combat the early "starving artist" narrative and quell the fear, I supplemented my income by freelancing as a florist. The learning curve was steep, but the process was fascinating. I met some great veteran freelancers who guided me through those early days. Looking back, I'm sure they saw me as a lost pup on job sites, but they helped me anyway.

As a bonus, and peek behind the curtain, here are a few quick lessons I learned from the freelance florist culture at the time.

### **<u>Floral Freelancing 101:</u>**

1) Never leave your clippers or knife lying around! They'll vanish, especially at events with a "cast of thousands." Nothing's more embarrassing than having to ask for a spare tool when everyone's under an intense deadline; a lived experience.

    ***Side Note:*** *Carry an extra, old set of tools for when this inevitably happens. If you're feeling generous, you can share them, but <u>don't expect to get them back.</u>*

2) Bring your own water or a refillable bottle.

3) Wear comfortable shoes. No open-toe shoes! You'll likely be on your feet for 10+ hours, often up and down ladders.

4) Pack snacks or a light lunch. Sometimes, the company doesn't feed you, and you may be transported out to the middle of nowhere with no nearby stores.

5) Track your hours and invoice immediately. As a subcontractor, it's your responsibility to bill the company; there are no punch cards for this!

    ***Side Note:*** *Get the complete billing info before you even step on-site. "I'm supposed to send my invoice to Suzie?" doesn't get you paid.*

6) Keep your bag in a safe place or, better yet, within eyesight at all times.

7) Bring Personal Protective Equipment: Gloves, band-aids, ointment, and safety glasses. You'll thank me later, especially when you're trimming branches on a ladder with pollen, thorns, and berries flying everywhere.

8) Limit bookings to 3 days per company. The whole reason you're freelancing is for flexibility, not to get sucked into company drama.

   ***Side Note:*** *The saying "After three days, fish and guests begin to stink" definitely applies.*

9) Be selective about the companies you work for. Do your research, and like with doctors, get a second opinion. Freelancers tend to look out for one another, so ask around for horror stories.

10) Show up, do your job, then leave. Don't get caught up in gossip. If you can, use earbuds. You're there to work, not network. (Though, secretly, it's both. But save the socializing for after-hours.)


I mention all this because, over time, I gradually transitioned from supplementing my business with freelancing to running it entirely on my own. Along the way, I found myself stepping into increasingly more leadership roles with clients or collaborators, as well as with freelancers I was now hiring, guiding, and relying on.

Freelancing ultimately improved my leadership in my own company, especially when it came to understanding the needs of freelancers. Likewise, the money I earned covered my living expenses while my business grew slowly. I was eventually able to cherry-pick the best freelance jobs with the best companies, the ones with great policies, fun crews, and the best lunches. Those years proved invaluable as I grew.

About seven years in, my business was established enough that I could quit freelancing altogether. Let me tell you, it was a massive shock to my finances. I knew I was "supplementing" my company with free-lance funds, but I hadn't realized just how much. Back taxes and credit card debt made for some lean times after the full pivot. Eventually, I re-structured my billing, expenses, and business plan, which helped me re-cover.

**Loosen the Reins:**

There have been times when I struggled to lift myself out of difficult situations, but over time, I've learned to ask for help. My Tejano pride and my own *Pinche Machismo* have often made this challenging. Even so, every time I've reached out for help, the empathy I've received has deeply moved me. In a world where the news and social media often focus on division and negativity, I find a reminder of the goodness of humanity in my daily practice.

When managing large-scale projects, there are moments when leaders must step back from the role of the sole creator, seek support from their team, and trust that the job will be accomplished.

One of the toughest lessons I've learned is letting go of my ego's desire to micromanage every task. And, I've come to understand that sometimes, good enough is enough to push a project forward. This extends to my team, as I've realized that no one will approach tasks exactly the way I would.

Many entrepreneurs start businesses because they are "rock stars" in their fields. However, being a "rock star" and running a business are two very different endeavors.

Shifting from a perfectionist mindset to a facilitator of growth was not an instantaneous process. It required loosening my grip on control and embracing imperfection. Over time, I really started to appreciate the process as much as the end result. I believe that genuine leadership is not about being perfect all the time but about fostering resilience, creativity, and trust within a team.

This shift hasn't been easy, especially with the fear of losing business always in the back of my mind. But it's a necessary step toward collective growth and progress. And again, nothing significant can be accomplished without the help of others.

**K.I.S.S.:**

Piggybacking on this frame of mind, when it comes to creating on a large scale, I've learned: Keep It Super Simple.

No one will do what you do and how you do it, and while this is a considerable strength, it can also be a significant weakness. Don't let it become a burden. When designing florals for large-scale events or monumental installations, I've trained myself to make my designs:

1) Easily explainable.
2) Simple enough that anyone can produce them.

**For aspiring event florists, please reread these two points and reflect on them, because they are crucial.**

It took me considerable time and effort to understand this on my own, but once I did, it made all the difference. This is also a great point to stop and remember the lessons from that introductory story, that the 'work' is never ours alone.

In large-scale productions, there are many moving parts, and our crews are made up of people with varied strengths and talents. While I'd love for my top players to contribute to every critical task, that's rarely possible. This is especially true because I want to keep them around for as long as possible (more on this in a bit). It means I don't always know who will be called away to deal with unexpected challenges. In those moments, a helper might need to step up and become a designer. This is why tasks need to be easily explainable and simple enough for anyone to produce.

Yes, I'm making it sound simpler than it actually is, and yes, there's a certain amount of experience required to truly understand what I'm saying here. However, when those instances arise, it will all make perfect sense.

When planning large events, it's important to accept that things won't go perfectly. Letting go of perfectionism has been a key lesson I've learned, which is why I keep emphasizing it.

**Trust:**

Ultimately, when working with a team, it comes down to trust. I need to trust that my crew is doing their best. While there will always be areas for improvement, I must treat others with the same respect and helpfulness I expect from them...the Golden Rule. Additionally, I have discovered something subtle yet miraculous. By trusting the crew and allowing them to learn as they go, many team members, especially newcomers, may experience freedom, trust, and authority over their work for the first time.

I often see fear in new members' initial attempts or first experiences with my crew, a fear that they might mess it up. However, by fostering a safe environment where mistakes can occur and be corrected without harsh judgment, they eventually come out of their shells. It is incredible to witness. I've noticed that by giving them that level of creative freedom, they naturally perform at their best and self-regulate according to the group's standards.

**They ALL Leave, By Design:**

This brings us back to an earlier point about keeping good help: YOU DON'T. Your "superstars" will almost invariably leave to pursue their own growth and development. That's just part of life, and our time with them is always limited. Accepting this was difficult for me at first, and even harder not to take personally. Now, when I hire contractors, I do so with this understanding. I train them, share my practices, and embrace the fact that they will eventually move on. It's all part of the process, nurturing talent, not to keep it, but to help it grow. Creatives need both roots and wings, the same as I did.

As floral event designers, we become practiced in knowing and carefully organizing where each floral arrangement will be placed in a space. The same can be said for a leader who thoughtfully manages the elements of team management, project uncertainties, and guides their team through chaos. Patience with customers and colleagues, shifting perspectives when needed, and knowing when to ask for help are all essential parts of the process. We've seen how assembling a positive team and creating a safe learning environment can make a big difference. Just as a complex installation is designed to look seamless, our tasks should be organized so they're easy for everyone on the team to understand and manage.

As we conclude this chapter, remember that authentic leadership promotes progress and growth, and avoids cramming our perfectionism on our teams. My focus has consistently been on cultivating an environment where all individuals are empowered to contribute to our collective success and to prosper with their own unique capabilities.

This shift from chasing perfection to facilitating collective growth reminds us that, despite the pressures of holding onto high standards and business demands, we're all works in progress. This, at its core, is the heart of leadership in floral design, art, and life.

And like dandelions scattering their seeds in the wind, we, as leaders, whisper our hopes, wishes, dreams, stories, and knowledge into them. And in doing so, we may find that we are not the keepers of the garden at all. Perhaps, instead, we are the wind itself. Scattering those dancing seeds of hope and story, trusting they will find their own ground and grow where our hands alone could never reach.

## Reflections:

- Have you ever considered leadership as part of your creative identity?

- What's your relationship to leadership? Does the word trigger anything in you?

- How do you balance your own spotlight with empowering others?

- How has perfectionism or over-control shown up in your work?

# 8

# FAILURE

We cannot advance in life without experiencing failure, and sometimes it feels never-ending. One example that immediately comes to mind is when I was learning to weld. I took the class initially because I had tasked myself to make a set of simple, albeit oversized, modern pedestals for an upcoming Lincoln Center gala. I made four large pieces that came out passable, a little wonky, but perfectly ok once filled with florals. Then, towards the end of the course study, I made two more, much smaller pieces that were rushed because I was short on time and funds. The instructor provided me with valuable advice on tackling the project, including the use of jigs made from wood to create an efficient workflow and tips on improving mechanics. Of course, what I heard was, "If you spend more money and time, you'll get a bit better results." Well, I winged it, and the resulting pedestals were a bit more parallelogram than rectangular; alas, I was out of time.

For the event, I dressed the smaller ones up by draping them in fabric, and thought that if I got a set of lovely planters, people would not notice the pedestals. Without doing any weight tests on the pedestals, I sent them out to use on-site. They were intended to live on stage where a Queen of Soul would perform that night. When we placed the planters I purchased on the pedestals, they started to wobble. "Crap!" I thought and quickly told my crew to pull those pedestals immediately and use the planters on the floor flanking the stage. Not a moment after I gave the crew instructions, a Union guy came up and started berating me, "You can NOT use those wobbly pedestals up there. That's a safety concern."... and on, and on, he went.... "That'll fall off the stage! What are you thinking? Are you trying to kill someone?" I feel like those are the moments that that particular guy waits for in every event when he can catch a failure and lay into someone. I explained I had already told my crew to get the pedestals out of the building, and the ceramic planters would live on the floor, not the stage. He huffed and puffed away, relaying what had happened to more Union workers as he went.

After my experience, I was motivated to learn more about the best practices for creating sturdy square pedestals. Part of it was a middle finger to the Union stagehand who made my day harder, but it was also to prove to myself that I was indeed dedicated to my craft. In a later continuing-ed welding class, I completed a set of four steel pedestals for a commissioned project. They turned out square, strong, and sexy. Ultimately, I had to create a wooden jig, as initially suggested, to achieve that level of quality. This experience made me realize that sometimes, I have been given the right advice but have failed to act on it. I guess, occasionally, it takes failing to learn the lesson and understand what I have already been told.

**A rose blooms from what is essentially a thorn bush. Do not mistake the winter thorns for the rose that has yet to come.**

One early spring day, I thought of this while clipping back climbing roses in a client's garden. The buds were only just beginning to swell.

Truthfully, it may have been a bit too early to cut them back, but private gardening rarely allows for perfect timing. So there I was, threading my arms through the prickly stalks, marveling at how these harsh, almost hostile branches would soon transform into lush foliage-filled stems with hundreds of fragrant, open blooms.

Failure can feel like my arms and hands after the seasonal tending of those thorns, all scraped up, cuts stinging, and disappointment seeping in, just like the blood that stains my bandages. But on the creative path, failure is unavoidable. The question is not if it will happen, but how we will meet it. That is where this chapter begins, working through the failing and finding the courage to keep going.

We all encounter failure early. A bike is usually the first classroom. The wobble, the crash, the pain of chalky white caliche gravel on skin. If we're lucky, someone's there to scoop us up, press a *besito*, a kiss to the wound, and whisper *"Sana sana colita de rana, dame un besito para hoy y mañana."* That peculiar little prayer that somehow eases the pain. A ritual so simple it seems magical. Then back on the seat we go, our knees burning, our arms stiff, until one day the balance takes hold, and somewhere along the way the training wheels come off. The crashes don't stop; in fact, they often multiply. But the joy outweighs the sting, and that freedom, the wind in our face, is enough to keep us riding. And once fully learned, it is never lost.

I've come to see failure in much the same way. It isn't a verdict unless we fully quit. It's a tally of the small wounds, tiny (sometimes large) scars that tell our story. The difference often comes down to the number of times I've been willing to stand back up, dust off, pick the muck out of my palms, and try again. People call it persistence, or grit, or even the law of averages. I don't know. For me, it's always been just a stubborn return to what I'm working towards.

Failure has been one of my most devoted teachers. Not kind, but consistent. It's forced me to take notice, recalibrate, swallow my pride, and start over, and over and over again. And though I could tell you a hundred small stories, in this chapter I want to take you inside one in particular. It comes in the epoch in my life we have been circling in this book, and here we dive into the summer I spent canvassing in Chicago. In this period, failure wasn't just a possibility; it was the daily air I breathed.

**Canvassing Chi-Town:**

The summer that followed my leaving, the School of the Art Institute of Chicago, I needed to find a job and do so quickly. Luckily, I found a shared sublet in a swanky Lake Shore Drive high-rise, just down the street. I got the place from a fellow School of the Art Institute of Chicago student whose best friend and roommate left the lease early to save money by moving back home for three months. During that summer, I relied on the sales and blue-collar skills I had learned while helping my mother in her shop, this time without the training wheels.

I quickly found a job as a canvasser for PeaceAction. It was one of the only jobs I was qualified for, and the ad said they'd provide "On-the-job, real-world training with the ability to enjoy the outdoors in beautiful Chicagoland." I didn't know what I was getting into, but they hired me... so off I went. A canvasser, if you're not familiar with the term, is that person who often looks like a young hippy standing in front of grocery stores or the middle of the sidewalks in major cities with a clipboard asking you rhetorical questions like "Do you love the planet?" or "Do you think we should protect our children?" As a 20-year-old, I was one of them. To be clear, this IS a job I would recommend to anyone with zero experience, particularly if someone is as lost as I was back then. What I learned on that job about failure and success, energy, putting in the legwork, and trusting oneself began molding me. It also taught me a lot about human nature.

When I started, they gave me the whole speech of do's and don'ts in the most ultra-passive-aggressive, liberal, and inclusive tone possible, which was way out of my comfort zone. And, yes, I'm saying this even though I was an art school dropout, a stoner who dressed like a vagabond with thrift store clothes I found in the discount bins. Getting past the "down with capitalism," "be peaceful always," and "let's change the planet together" jargon, we learned our field rap, which would be fundamental to the season's membership drive. We were paid slightly over minimum wage, around seven dollars an hour at the time, but we would get bonuses based on the number of members we signed up weekly. In the summer of 1997, the campaign was based on lobbying Congress to sign the landmines treaty ban. We were given a script to study. The more information we memorized from the script, the more facts we'd have to work with in case someone decided to challenge or question us. If they didn't donate or become a member, it was our job to at least get a signature…because that was the minimum requirement to establish political clout.

Our rap for out in the field started with, "Are you against landmines? (Wait for the YES…then proceed) "Do you know about Princess Diana and her recent walk through the landmine fields of Angola?" Bear in mind here that I could hardly remember any of the facts. Half the time, I couldn't even remember it was Princess <u>Diana</u> who was the lead-in to our rap. Often I'd say, "You know the Princess?" Boy, was I unfocused and unmotivated! I only wanted to be in the studio painting, not hearing about how everything I was saying was offensive, how the world was on fire, or that nearly everything I had been taught and how I've been living was wrong. So, yes, my rap sucked!

Anyway, the time quickly came to hit the streets, and the people who still didn't have a grasp of the rap (Me!) were sent to the sidewalks of the Magnificent Mile to sign up members, collect donations, get signatures, or, in my case, simply pass out information pamphlets. I made it my personal mission to blow through those pamphlets as quickly as possible so I could call it a day, go home, and make art.

*ProTip: No one takes a pamphlet from you if you are handing it to them with squared-up shoulders and straight toward someone's chest; if you can imagine the way a cop might hand you a ticket. However, if you pop it out, BAM! Towards them, as they walk by, low and slick where their hands naturally are…you gotta imagine the drug deal money exchange scene in a cheesy old movie. This style of delivery works!…. They'll most likely take it, at least on the streets of Chicago.*

After about a week, we were finally sent out to the suburbs of Chicago to canvas for the membership drive. The veterans told me that this is where the real bonus money would start coming in. It wouldn't be easy, though. We were racing to cover new territory fast because our competitor, Greenpeace, was hitting the suburbs hard that summer. I was told not to get into prolonged debates with people because the time we had in the day was limited, and we had to call it quits at sundown.

We were assigned to teams of two, and we had to watch out for each other. This was a top priority because some people we'd come across would get extremely angry and even hostile when disturbed by strangers. So, there I was, knocking on doors and going through my rap, that is, if I could even get two words in before the door slammed. Getting to the stage where I'd at least ask for the signature or a donation was a win. Honestly, the first week was a hot mess. I don't think I got one membership and hardly any signatures, for that matter. It was rejection after rejection. Whenever I did get someone to let me start my rap, I was so flabbergasted my mind often would go blank, and I would forget why I was even there...so a signature drive it quickly became for me.

Daily, my partner and I would find a shady spot to eat our lightly packed lunch of a bit of fruit or some nuts. We'd then go over how we were doing. We noticed <u>it was all about energy</u>. Getting rejected over and over chipped away at our energy, especially when the rejection came with someone screaming in our faces. Still, we had to encourage ourselves to stay upbeat, because every encounter carried the hope that the next person might just be a future member.

> **Side Bar:** *A funny and admittedly gross story of something else I learned that summer is: "Anything you put in your body needs to come out." So we quickly learned to eat light. Oranges and apples worked well. Maybe a handful of nuts, and I learned to consume as <u>little water</u> as needed. This was vital knowledge, especially in those upper-class neighborhoods, where if you could get anyone to answer, it was HIGH-LY unlikely they'd let you use their restroom. One such afternoon, early in our canvassing, we were in Oak Park. No one was answering their*

*doors. It was an abysmal day. I had too much water to drink and couldn't hold it anymore. So, the Texan in me told my partner to be the lookout while I went into the bush. I finished up, and we headed off. As we rounded the corner, we simultaneously realized I'd just pissed on a famous Frank Lloyd Wright House! So yeah, that happened. I'm not proud of it, but I am also a bit amused at my ignorance sometimes.*

Each suburb and neighborhood was different. This is exactly what Chicago is known for; it isn't called the "City of Neighborhoods" for nothing. It varies even from block to block. Eventually, we made it back into the city to canvas there. Strategically, the managers waited two weeks after they knew that Greenpeace had passed through before sending us out to any particular area. The most successful neighbors in the city and the suburbs were the Middle to Upper-Middle class. This was a total surprise to me. I thought places like Lake Forest and Waukegan, with their massive homes, would be the most significant donors....nope!  And as I would later learn in NYC working in the Non-Profit Gala arena, this subset of individuals makes their donations at these large events after they've been wined and dined first...and, of course, while admiring all the spectacular flowers!

One day, we were sent out to one of these neighborhoods, specifically the Northern Suburbs of Winnetka, made famous in the movie *Home Alone*. The homes and properties in this neighborhood were vast, with only six or eight properties per block. It was eerie to be there midday, midweek, silent, vacant, with only the sounds of gardeners' leaf blowers resonating in the distance. That day, a singular housekeeper answered the door and let me in to speak to her boss personally.

Let me back up here. From the outside, the home was of the typical English Manor style standard in the area, with ancient trees in the front lawn towering above the three-story mansion. Making my way up the circuitous inclined walkway towards the front door, my heart fluttered. "This is it," I thought, "the moment I would finally get a yearly membership."

Once inside, I was blown away by the interior of their home. It was the first time I had ever been in a home like that. Sure, I had been in 'rich people homes' (or interchangeably 'white people homes' in Alicean vernacular) back in Alice, Texas, but this one made those look like a pool house. Everything was grand, spotless, and aglow from the ambient light filtering through the oversized windows. The echoing of heels on the highly polished, mirror-finished marble tiles resonated through the cavernous vestibule as the owner approached, methodically dust-testing surfaces as she made her way. The moment she saw me, she immediately spun around on those heels and instructed the housekeeper, with a shooing flick of a wrist, "Offer him some water and escort him out." Her echoing voice from a distant doorway spoke out, "We make all our donations directly with the organizations we support at the end of the year!" The housekeeper escorted me to the back door as she grabbed a tiny water bottle out of the SubZero refrigerator, muttering *"¿Qué podemos hacer?...Así es...Buena suerte."* Deflated, head down, staring at my feet, I slowly made my way down the long-sloping driveway in wonderment at what I had just experienced.

At the other end of the spectrum, people didn't have extra money to donate if their income bracket was too low. Also, in lower-income neighborhoods, people are highly skeptical and don't trust putting their name on anything, so good luck getting a signature from them. Additionally, instead of an annoyed person answering the door, it was more likely that a snarling pit bull would greet you rather than a person.

I was familiar with this bracket. I had lived my entire life in it....Hell, I was still living it! In addition to earning enough money to pay rent, I also worked every week to earn extra cash for my Sunday Dinner. Depending on how my week went, I would treat myself to Ronny's $7.99 steak dinner on Randolph Street in the Loop, or it'd be a couple of packs of six-for-a-dollar Ramen noodles.

On bad days, I'd walk home from the office with my head down, staring into the cracks of the sidewalk, feeling invisible and utterly spent. I was so low that even people experiencing homelessness would stop me to offer a few kind words or share what little they could to lift my spirits.

Sometimes, it felt like they were the only people I'd connect with all day. Some would hand me a free postcard they'd picked up from kiosks in the city, the kind they usually resold to tourists for spare change. I held onto those postcards like small treasures. I'd write to my mom on them, telling her how great things were going, how I was still chasing my dreams, and how my art career was just about to take off. I didn't want her to worry. She didn't need to know how lost I was or how deeply unseen I felt by a world I was so desperate to be part of.

There I was day after day, putting in miles and returning to the office with whatever donations I gathered, ten or twenty dollars max. Eventually, that summer, they brought in a hot-shot canvasser from LA, the top fundraiser in the West Coast Region. He was a short, grungy, charismatic guy, full of cocky angst and bravado. Everyone on the team recognized early, he loved it when he would get the comparisons to Zac de la Rocha of Rage Against the Machine (a band extremely popular at the time). We were told he was there to teach us better sales pitches and techniques. However, after a few days in the field, he was producing relatively the same numbers as we were. One night on the ride home, he admitted defeatedly, "Man, these areas are hard! Did they get hit already by other canvassers or something? Back home, we tell people where we are from, and they sign up for full memberships. I don't even need to go into a full rap half the time. Don't you all have any renewals we can hit?" The rest of the team was in the back of the station wagon, sharing smirks with each other as he said so. We all already knew what, he quickly learned that NOTHING is that easy...at least not in the Windy City! They make you work for everything.

After six weeks, I was physically and emotionally exhausted from the doors slamming in my face. I finally broke. I had had enough! I got to this one house, rang the bell, and as soon as he answered the door, the man started, "Oh no, no, no......." I interrupted immediately, "My NAME IS JUAN, AND I AM A HUMAN BEING!!" This threw the man way off...I remember the guy took a step back. "I'm out here in this heat, sweating my ass off, working to save kids from being BLOWN UP!" I went into my rap, only this time in my own words. I remember the person didn't become a member, but he gave me a ten-dollar donation and offered me a rare glass of water. Although we were forbidden to take non-bottled water, lest we get roofied, I took it as a win because of the sentiment.

After that, the tide began to change, primarily due to a course correction in my mind. My rap became frank. I relaxed my tone; when appropriate, I'd even crack jokes if I thought that would resonate. I started having fun with the people and not taking it so seriously and <u>personally</u>.

I was getting into my flow in those last days of the canvas. It indeed became a game of numbers for me. If I got a no, fine, I would quickly move on to the next door. I mean, I began moving along at a light jogger's pace. If the conversation started to get prolonged, I would quickly explain to them, "I must keep moving on and hit more homes because this is how, as a group, we can most efficiently effect change." Then, I would leave them with a brochure with my name to have them call the office directly if they changed their minds. Then, I'd quickly be on my way. I kept telling myself, "Every No gets me one person closer to a Yes." Regularly, the managers would have to come to pull me and my partner from the field because it was getting too dark. We had become laser-focused on keeping up positive energy and, at the same time, hitting as many homes as possible.

At the end of the summer campaign with PeaceAction, I luckily found a new job at the Viacom Super Store. My roommate was already working in the Nickelodeon department as their superstar; he vouched for me, which helped me get the job in the MTV department.

That summer taught me numerous life lessons, mostly about myself and my potential, when I trusted my instincts. My confidence grew, and I did learn about the neighborhoods and people of Chicago. I realized the locals were not interested in any BS, but they were willing to lend a hand if they saw you were determined to achieve the goals you sincerely believed in. And, yes, I did begin regularly signing people up for annual memberships. Although I wouldn't win any door-to-door salesman awards, I discovered I could sell. It was all about connecting with the person you were speaking to on an emotional level rather than bombarding them with statistics and numbers.

I also found out some people don't answer the door or allow you to speak because they know if you hit the right chord with them, they won't be able to resist signing up...those big, guarded softies. Finally, there was the type that never had any intention of signing up but loved the tit-for-tat of discussion and debate that would suck the life, time, and momentum from the focused goal.

Even though it often felt like we were facing rejection after rejection, it was only a temporary part of the process. More importantly, each failure forced us to evaluate why it was happening and make adjustments, often the smallest ones (a word, a glance, an inflection point) that could completely change the outcome next time. Sometimes, it was as simple as turning the wheels a bit faster to find that balance, to catch that momentum, which would keep you upright and moving forward. The key was in the analysis. Through this, I learned an essential truth that the difference between success and failure often comes down to tiny, deliberate tweaks. And it was in those small shifts that all the difference was made. This insight, simple as it may seem, has remained one of the most valuable lessons of my career.

Failures, much like the harsh winter, can seem endless and unforgiving. Just as winter yields to the vibrant blooms of spring, failure is often a stepping stone to success. When you first ride a bike, you are bound to fall. This is only a momentary reflection of your ability, and is a necessary step in the learning process. The law of averages ensures that success is inevitable if we begin making gradual adjustments in our strategy and if we persist. My big takeaway as a door-to-door canvasser in Chicago is that each rejection brings us closer to a 'yes,' and likewise, each failure brings us closer to our goals. Subtle, incremental shifts, even though seemingly insignificant, change the trajectory, leading to substantial growth over time.

It is also essential, sometimes, to tear up the script we've been handed and speak from the heart to connect with our audience. Learning to recognize good advice can sometimes be subtle, and its importance might not be obvious at first. However, over time and upon reflection, its true value often becomes clear.

Remember that our failures do not define us, nor are we alone or immune to experiencing them. They are, after all, a universal part of the human experience.

---

## Reflections:

– How has failure, the great equalizer, shown up as a teacher in your life?

– What does your version of "putting in the numbers" look like?

– When you're unsure of direction, where do you turn?

# 9

## INTENTION

Growing up, we lived through countless seasons of poverty. It wasn't easy. In hindsight, it served as my training ground for handling adversity. My family surrounded me, and I felt loved; at the same time, I don't nostalgically romanticize those times. Because I also remember standing in long lines as a child, under the brutal sun, waiting for essentials like cheese, peanut butter, milk, and bread. My mother worked tirelessly, often taking on double shifts and sometimes even two or three jobs at once, to ensure we had what we needed. She made it look effortless from the outside, but I know now the weight she carried. There were stretches where she was little more than a passing shadow in our home, a *fantasma*, appearing briefly as the sun rose, before heading back out to work. I remember often leaving notes for her on the dining table to catch up and let her know what was going on in my life. And yet, despite her exhaustion, she somehow kept us on track, ensuring we stayed focused on school.

That experience of lack isn't unique when poverty is involved, but I've realized it extends beyond economics; it's cultural, too. When I think about Tejano heroes and sheroes, I can count the prominent ones on one or two hands. Growing up, I didn't know a single fine artist from South Texas. It wasn't until I arrived in Chicago that I learned they existed.

At my core, I believe that as an artist examining the Tejano diaspora, I can help shift this narrative. Our story, the story of *Mi Gente*, the multi-generational Texans of Mexican descent, deserves to be seen, heard, and valued. We have always been here, enduring, adapting, and thriving despite the odds. Like the mesquite tree, our roots run deep, our branches reaching outward to embrace new light and new possibilities. Our lives and stories matter. And by sharing my experiences, I claim space for us in places that have too long ignored or overlooked our contributions.

But being the change I want to see has come with sacrifices, a reality that is at the heart of intention and discipline. Some might see my decisions as selfish, given the time spent away from family, birthdays, and holidays missed. And they are trade-offs. The guilt and shame of not being there with my loved ones is real, and they burn deep. But pursuing my ambitions meant choosing a different path than the one expected of me.

Growing up, many young men saw two options for survival: enlist in the military or work in the oil fields. Both are honorable and worthy of full respect. But I wanted something different. My heart called to make art. For me, staying would have meant silencing that voice, and I simply couldn't.

I also learned early on that my name alone, Juan, carried a weight in Texas that felt different from what it should have. That's why, at home, I became J.M. It was a mask, a subtle shift meant to subvert the shame pressed on me. When I left, it was to find a place where I didn't feel like I had to justify my existence in America, even though my family has been here for generations. I was searching for a place where I could feel welcomed, not merely tolerated. I was tired of smiling and gently nodding, as my tongue bled underneath. All in service of pleasing others. This was exactly the type of discipline I WAS abandoning. In truth, I didn't know where I was headed or if I'd ever return. And while I see things changing in Texas, with new voices rising and more representation, I've come to understand the work I need to do now requires other soil.

So, even when I'm designing floral installations in New York City, I am thinking about them. Every painting, sculpture, garden, and floral piece I create carries threads back to my roots. My work is a love letter to my past, to the people who shaped me, to a future where we don't have to fight to be recognized.

This is the path that has led me to my *why*. I create for myself, for my family, for my community, for *Mi Raza*, and for anyone who has ever been made to feel unseen or undervalued. I invite those who have ever longed for home, and knowing they may never return, to sit with me. Hear these words you may have kept folded in your pocket and close to your wounded heart. Turn up the volume until you can hear yourself resonating in them again.

Ultimately, I want children growing up in places like Alice, Texas, to know they have options, and their worth isn't tied to what they can endure. I want them to know that they are more than what society has predetermined for them. And that they never, not for a second, have to accept being made to feel less than, less than intelligent, less than worthy because of their name, their skin, or the circumstances they were born into.

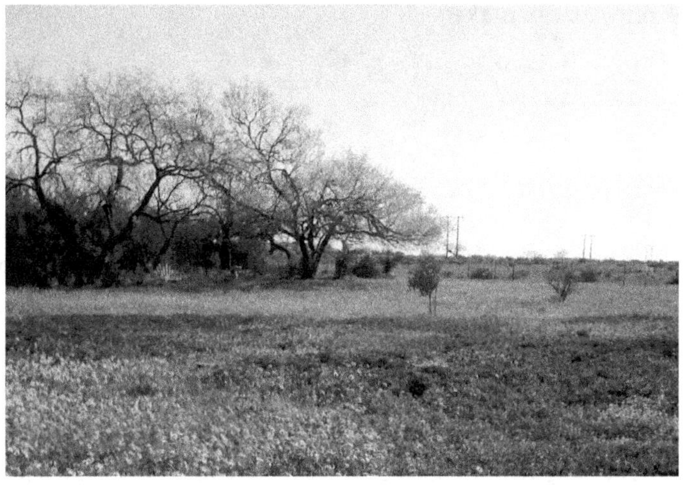

Pastures at my family's ranch in South Texas. Photo by me.

**Acts of Faith:**

Leaving Texas was an act of hope and faith. I was chasing a life where I could define myself on my own terms. That choice was intentional, and it required a kind of discipline, but not the kind rooted in punishment. This discipline is about devotion and showing up for what truly matters, even when it's hard.

In this chapter, I want to explore how intention shapes our practice, not as abstract ideals, but as choices we make daily, often internally, in the face of uncertainty.

As creatives, we often hear about "following our passions," but the truth is less glamorous. I've found it's about showing up in our own lives, guided by our values, persevering when the odds are stacked, and making decisions that honor the long view over the much easier quick win.

Diversifying my work has been part of that practice. I've moved across mediums, shifted when necessary, and refused to box myself in. Each path taught me something, and each small step built toward something larger. Along the way, I've often asked: "Am I shaping my goals, or are my actions shaping me?" The answer shifts with time, but the lesson remains: the creative life is an act of faith in uncertainty.

Intention, discipline, and creativity aren't at odds. They are companions, each sharpening the other, guiding us through the unknown toward the work only we can make.

**Deliver the Goods:**

My life has taught me the importance of discipline through all the challenges to my core values, which has also played a key role in sharpening my artistic skills. Still, providing high-quality work and applying practical solutions during these moments have been my main priorities. Anything less can jeopardize a career. The fact of the matter is, sending out shit work will eventually end your career and likely end it quickly. We all have bad days, and I have sent out work that I wish I could get back. In the past, struggling to deliver consistent work was an Achilles' heel.

I began addressing this in my business practice by evaluating the standards I've set for myself and my clients' expectations. This structure guides my critique of the work based on these standards and expectations. Admittedly, I had problems maintaining my standards when I started my business. Remember when I began, I was also freelancing and working a string of 10-hour days in a row, then getting a last-minute order for my own company, I would be too burnt out to deliver my best work.

I remember one distinct occasion when I received an order for a last-minute gift arrangement from one of my best clients, but with another freelance gig scheduled later in the morning, I phoned it in. What I sent out was a bunch of garden roses in a cylinder. Don't get me wrong, the roses were fresh and stunning, oh, how I do love a garden rose! But they are not what I am known for. Also, I had run out of my fancy packing materials, so it went out with simple tissue paper to protect the flowers. It lacked in the packing, all the personalized, handmade touches I like to include. I felt horrible after sending it out. Nevertheless, I had a freelance job I had to get to. The problem, I later realized, was that having it happen once was the impetus to making it a little easier the next time.

The secret to changing this behavior was catching it immediately when I noticed it happening again. I started telling myself, "No! My clients come to me and expect a certain standard. It is a privilege and an honor to produce work for them. They've put their trust in me to fulfill this order, and it's up to me to show my respect for doing so." Again, catching it as it was happening was the key.

**Identifying My Standards:**

Moments when my standards were not quite right raised the question: Am I procrastinating, lazy, or burnt out? And we've already covered how to recognize and answer those questions. Suppose the answer is no to all of them. Then, what is causing this inconsistency in my work, such as missed deadlines or decreased quality? To answer this question, I needed to do some real soul-searching and be humble enough to confront the truth. As an artist and business owner, I take full ownership and responsibility for my work. I am committed to identifying and addressing these inconsistencies to uphold my and my client's standards.

I don't strive for average in any of these matters; my goal is excellence, even when dog-tired. We owe it to ourselves, our clients, and our craft. This sentiment isn't just limited to what we create; it's also about how we make it. I also expect the team I work with to have great attitudes and innovative ideas, and to be consistently interested in improving in all areas of their lives. I want a team that brings something unique to the table, helping us all grow and achieve more. I don't expect them to stay the same; I want them to evolve and enhance their skills, knowing that greatness resides within them.

**Know The Client:**

One of the most important factors in any floral project is that they are time-sensitive. Every arrangement, installation, or event must progress, develop, and be completed with intent. This isn't merely internal dialogue. I lay it out clearly with clients from the very start, just as I discussed in the chapter on respect. My commitment is that each project is completed on time, every time, to the highest standard.

Equally essential is understanding who you're creating for, what their taste, needs, and definition of beauty are. One recent project reminded me just how transformative it can be when you really get your client. An ivy wall installation that began as a simple concept evolved into something far more layered, as you'll read.

**Ivy Walls:**

A colleague of mine, an old friend from my freelance days, had a long-time client who needed a large-scale floral installation for their home. The deadline was tight, and the project had to be completed before a major architectural magazine arrived for a photoshoot. Due to my friend's unavailability, I was brought in as a subcontractor by the lead designer of the shoot, a renowned figure within the industry, to help execute the vision.

During our initial walk-through, the client and I discussed their vision: a natural, aged look, with wisteria and ivy creeping up three sides of a 30-foot interior wall in a fully finished and impeccably furnished Greenwich Village carriage house. While some elements would be real, the majority of the materials would be faux, carefully selected to appear as organic as possible. After finalizing the design, I moved quickly to bring the project to life.

All went smoothly in the process, and when the installation was completed, I was pleased with the results. However, a week later, I received a call from the client asking us to return. They wanted the design to feel 'lighter' in both volume and color. A special note was added: the shoot was at the end of the week.

On the day we arrived to make adjustments, my colleague happened to be at the house, installing her weekly flowers. It was the first time she had seen the completed project. She took one look at the installation and immediately said, "This is stunning, but they are not going to like it."

I was caught off guard. "What do you mean?" I asked.

She explained, "They don't like dark, moody tones, and you've covered up all the twisted wisteria branches. Those are their favorite parts."

That was one of those moments when the power of long-term client relationships rang true and clear. My colleague had been working with this family for years. She knew their aesthetic preferences, from the overarching look to the smallest details. Over time, she had developed an understanding of their specific language around beauty, what they meant when they said "I'd like it lighter," how they interpreted color and space, and what they gravitated toward stylistically.

Her insight was invaluable. With her guidance, we adjusted the installation to reveal more of the wisteria's natural form and introduced softer, more delicate elements to balance the composition. Simple adjustments that would have taken us numerous trials to solve without her wise counsel. The client loved the final result.

That experience reinforced an important truth: having someone who deeply understands a client's evolving aesthetic, even as a second set of eyes, can make the difference between a good and a great project.

**Trust Yourself:**

Looking back, I realized the importance of trusting my instincts.

During the initial consultation, I walked through the space with the family, asked the right questions, and even created a 3D rendering that they had approved. But later, as the installation progressed, I started incorporating suggestions from the professionals who had brought me onto the project. While their input was well-intentioned, it ultimately led the design away from what the client had initially envisioned.

In the end, after all the adjustments, the final result looked nearly exactly like my original detailed rendering.

The lesson here was clear. Trust your instincts, and don't confuse them with emotional reactions. I've learned I must listen to my gut while remaining open to valuable input. The key is striking the right balance of making decisions rooted in both expertise and clear client communication. Had I trusted my initial approach, I could have saved time, effort, and revisions.

This experience reminded me that while collaboration is valuable, staying true to one's own trained intuition is just as critical. Sometimes, the best solution *is* the one you had all along.

**Don't Take it Personally?:**

As we transition from understanding client needs, we now turn our attention to another equally important aspect: managing situations without taking them personally. But how do we uphold our standards and seek assistance when needed without taking it personally?

Well, to be completely honest, I'm still learning not to take things personally; perhaps I've simply become adept at compartmentalizing, and often I am still biting my tongue...even if this is not the healthiest mode of dealing with emotions. A vital lesson I've learned over the years is to view client demands or critiques as driven by their needs rather than as a personal attack. While it can be challenging to overcome that initial feeling of rejection, professionalism must prevail. This is where my moral, ethical, and value-driven discipline comes into play. And yes, it sometimes feels like a delicate balancing act.

Understanding a client's distinct needs can be complicated. Initially, I start piecing their needs together by asking a lot of questions, paying close attention to their dress, their personality, and, if applicable, their home decor. Become like a detective as you search for clues, as you discover who the client is, what they are about, what they value, and how you can contribute more of this to their lives.

Our unique strengths as designers or creatives, such as a keen eye for detail and a fresh perspective, are invaluable in understanding and fulfilling client needs. Our ability to think quickly and adapt in crisis management is equally important. All this said, I also acknowledge that individuals' experiences, strengths, and weaknesses can vary greatly.

So, be open to seeking help or collaboration when needed. Actively leveraging our strengths and navigating the unique traits that make us wonderfully different are keys to successful relationships with our clients. Getting it right for your client also requires time, patience, and a humble approach. The reward comes in the loyalty you cultivate over time and the value you provide to your clients long term.

As I've deepened my relationship with discipline throughout my career, I've come to realize how much it relies on being intentional. The more I've clarified my purpose and values, the more naturally my boundaries formed around client expectations, business decisions, and creative standards. I've come to trust both my gut and my reason. These two voices of intuition and logic have guided me through uncertainty, especially when external markers of success or clarity were missing. Skill matters. So does knowledge. But neither means much without the inner compass to know when and how to use them.

I'm continually reminded that learning isn't linear, and it's a lifelong process. I've faced challenges that made me question my choices and the advice I've given. And I've had moments of joy and achievement that reminded me why I chose this path in the first place. All of it has shaped me. Discipline, real discipline, isn't a rigid rulebook. It's a lived practice. A way of moving through the world with intention, even when it's hard. Especially when it's hard.

---

## Reflections:

– In what ways do you meet the needs of your clients or community with intention?

– In what ways do you define your own standards, both personally and professionally?

– How has collaboration expanded or challenged your work?

# 10

## FEAR

"It all started when I was a child..." I tease, though, in many ways, it did.

I wasn't a particularly fearful child, but I wasn't reckless either. Let's say I enjoyed calculated risks. Growing up on the ranch gave me a freedom that, in hindsight, shaped my approach to fear. I would often be found climbing trees, running around the fifty-acre woods solo, jumping off my grandfather's trailer loaded with twenty-foot tall stacks of hay bales, or, most likely, playing with fire.

To this day, my family taunts me about it, saying, "The fire calls to you." They aren't wrong. Often, my mother would catch me in one of these acts, and her response was always the same: "*¡AY!* If you hurt yourself, I'm not taking you to the hospital! You're taking aspirin and crying yourself to sleep, *cabrón!*" And she meant it. I learned the hard way.

One day, while playing with fire in an old oil barrel, I grabbed a stick that was already smoldering. The pain was instant. Screaming, I ran back to the trailer, only to find myself alone in my room moments later, hand bandaged up, crying myself to sleep as the Tylenol took hold.

So, no, I wasn't a daredevil. But a risk-taker? Absolutely. And yes, my mother would have begrudgingly taken me to the hospital if needed, but I think what she was teaching me was that MY actions had real-life consequences...an extremely Tejana thing to do.

That same kind of tough love also appeared later when she started her own flower shop; it didn't turn into some magical financial cushion for our family. Keeping that small-town storefront alive took everything she had. It was a full-time act of endurance and devotion. So, even though we had each other, we all understood the unspoken rule early on: "You need to find your own way."

Winston Churchill once said, "If you're going through hell, keep going." I've come to understand just how right he was. Fear, doubt, jealousy, the sting of rejection, the creeping inner voice of negativity, these have been my silent companions for as long as I can remember. For years, they whispered from the shadows, influencing my choices in ways I couldn't yet understand. The naming of them was only the first step. The real work has been learning to move through them, strip away their power, and stop letting them define how I walk through the world.

My mission now is to break the cycle, to step out from under their weight and claim a life that isn't dictated by fear. Not to erase it but to transform it. To face the shadows not as an obstacle to escape, but as something to recognize and understand.

**Moving Toward Fears:**

I've also always been a bit of a loner and a dreamer, traits that may have stemmed from that childhood on the ranch. Unlike many, the fear of striking out on my own has never been a big deal for me, a quality that has undoubtedly contributed to my career success, and I have layered this with adapting to view fear differently along the way.

My core team has humorously dubbed me *"Juan sin miedo,"* or Juan without fear. I think it's because, during installations, I can often be heard saying, "Do not be afraid! Just begin adding flowers. If something is wrong, I'll tell you. *¡Házlo, no tengas miedo!* Do it. Don't be afraid."

It's become something of a mantra in my studio practice, a way to break the paralysis of perfectionism and a battle cry to push through those gnawing moments of self-doubt.

**Rewriting the Story:**

But this wasn't always the case. For years, I worked with a fire at my back, barely outrunning the fear of failure. It was always there, pressing against my ribs, a constant whisper that I was one misstep away from collapse. I let that fear drive me, let it shape me into someone who could withstand anything, who could take on more than I should, who could survive. And it was exhausting.

Fear, I found out, is a poor sculptor. It carves jagged, raw edges and leaves deep grooves where gentleness should be. I didn't know, then, that I was feeding a shadow I didn't have to obey.

I remember many occasions, standing in a studio late at night, hands stained with paint, exhaustion humming through my bones, staring starry-eyed, at a half-finished piece and thinking, "Is this enough? Am I enough?" That question followed me everywhere in the beginning. I thought success would mean silence and that the voice of doubt would vanish when I achieved enough, when I proved myself enough times. But no, it doesn't work that way. The fear doesn't leave; it only changes shape.

For a long time, I allowed fear to control my sense of worth. I was influenced by impossible self-imposed expectations and silent societal pressures, which shaped how I moved through the world. So, I worked harder. I achieved more. I kept pushing. But no amount of external validation could drown out that inner voice that whispers, "If they really knew you, they'd see you don't belong."

It took time, and pain, and loss, but I finally started to see the shape of the thing I had been running from. Like the Devil card in Tarot, fear tricks you into believing you're bound to it, when, in reality, the chains are loose. You only need to lift them off and walk away. The more I sat with it, the more I realized I wasn't running from failure. I was running from myself. From my own self-knowing. So I stopped. I turned and faced it. And in that moment, something shifted. I started painting with my shadow instead of against it. This realization came to a head during the period I previously mentioned, when I was creating works for the two-person show in Chicago.

**Painting with My Shadow:**

At that time, my life was anything but stable. Before I found the apartment that became my first live-in studio, I was barely getting by. I had just left my canvassing job with PeaceAction and started working retail at the MTV Viacom store. At the time, I was still living in that high-rise sublet on Lake Shore Drive, while my finances, emotions, and creativity were all starting to fray at the edges. Summer was ending, and with my bank account nearly empty, as I waited for the new pay to begin to kick in, I needed a permanent place to live.

When I say I was broke, I don't mean the kind of "broke" I saw at the School of the Art Institute of Chicago, where being out of money meant waiting for parental deposits to hit the account before another night out. My broke meant scraping up change for a few packs of ramen, or a Metro-Card, and a bank balance too low for an ATM withdrawal. Once, I even argued with my bank, asking how I could access my own money for food. They recommend I write myself a check for the pitiful amount left in my account.

So, when a landlady called about a budget-friendly artist's apartment, I jumped at the chance. A train and a bus ride later, I stepped into a rough, 1,200-square-foot, two-bedroom space. It was worn and raw, but it had promise. I ignored the neighborhood's warning signs, gunshots I'd later recognize as a nightly soundtrack, and signed the lease, too excited about finally having a space to create.

Reality hit on the way home. I had used my last transfer getting to the train, leaving me stranded with a four-hour walk back to the lake shore at night, with a route straight through Cabrini-Green, no less. So, I panhandled for train fare, my pride burning when a stranger muttered, "I hope I'm not buying you another fix." I didn't look like an artist wanting to get home; I looked like an addict.

Moving day came, and my former roommate's father begrudgingly helped me haul what little I owned: a couple of boxes, rolled canvases, paint supplies, and a Woolworth's rug. As soon as they dropped me off, I tacked canvases to the formal dining room walls and got to work. The adjoining sunroom was crumbling, the rooftop off the kitchen was a liability, and the windows needed plastic drop cloths to keep out the brutal Chicago winter. For my sleeping situation, I laid out the Woolworth's rug on the living room floor as my bed, rolled up clothes became a pillow, and my winter coat became a blanket.

Why the living room? The bedrooms freaked me out, and at least the amber street lights in the front room served as my makeshift nightlight in case I had nighttime intruders. Indeed, one night, I was woken up by a rat the size of a housecat gnawing at my toes, sending me scrambling to set up blinking Christmas lights surrounding my rug bed as a makeshift deterrent.

Apparently, my landlady noticed the struggle, having let herself in while I was at work, and left me a worn-out foam mattress she'd dug out of the basement. On it, she left a note that read: "It seemed like you could use this. I appreciate the art you're working on." It was a kindness and a reminder that privacy was a luxury I hadn't yet learned to demand.

Still, I painted every day, working late into the night, pushing through exhaustion, hunger, and fear. I mean, who could really sleep soundly, alone, in those conditions? The pieces I made for that show terrified me in many ways, confronting childhood trauma, mortality, and the abyss of my own mind. And yet, art was the only thing keeping me from slipping further. It was my salvation, even as the pursuit of it deepened my suffering.

Sleep deprivation, cheap wine, and malnutrition made my paranoia worse, but creating kept me anchored to something real, and my mind distracted during those long nights.

Things eventually shifted. A new roommate, a former SAIC student from Kenya, moved in, bringing with him pots, pans, a full set of furniture, and even a car. For the first time in months, I wasn't completely alone. I slowly cleaned up my life and built a small network of friends, people who saw me, understood me, and reminded me I wasn't invisible. And during this chaotic, transformative period, I met my now-wife. Falling in love, of course, terrified me, too. I second-guessed everything, even turning to tarot and I Ching readings to find validations for my feelings. Finally, a brutally honest friend sliced through my doubt: "We get maybe two or three true loves in a lifetime. Don't fuck this one up!" She'd always had a way with words.

Even with all this drama, the show, as I wrote about earlier, went well, and the work, the art, was a success, if only in my mind. It finally felt like I was turning a corner.

But life had another upheaval in store. The landlady sold the building, and we were forced to leave. The displacement was brutal, one more fracture in a season already splintered by instability. But the real upheaval wasn't the apartment. It was the beginning of the transmutation of the version of me who thought suffering was the price owed to make something meaningful. I look back on him now, and my heart aches. That younger version of me didn't know how to manage fear or protect his own softness. I thought the only way forward was through the fire. And to keep getting burned.

Even then, art never left my side. I was sacrificing for it, and in return, it was what kept pulling me through. It was an ever-present lifeline I could follow when everything else fell away.

**Seeing the Shift:**

In hindsight, I see how truly blessed I have been, despite moments of immense struggle. Poverty, displacement, and uncertainty shaped much of that time after leaving home. These experiences are all too well-known for many in the Latino community. But within all that chaos, I found breakthroughs in my art and myself. Each step forward required shedding an old version of who I thought I was, stripping away layers of ego, self-doubt, and fear. And that's where I found something raw and true at the center of it all.

Letting go of parts of my ego wasn't easy. Fear and anger still clung to me, whispering all the reasons why I wasn't good enough, why I should stop, why I should play it safe. But when I leaned into that fear instead of resisting it, something shifted. My art became more honest, and my process more fluid, more vital. I was no longer painting to prove something; I was simply creating. I began to see my work as an extension of myself rather than an attempt to impress or conform. The pieces I created during that time weren't always polished, but they were real. They carried the weight of my experiences, my struggles, and my transformation. And that truth resonated deeply in ways I hadn't anticipated.

Speaking on this kind of artistic reckoning doesn't happen easily. It's a painful process of peeling back the layers and wounds, unlearning old narratives, so we can open up space for something new to emerge. I had to confront my fears and my own complicity in limiting myself. The world had told me who I was supposed to be, what I was supposed to want, and how I was supposed to create. And before the shift, I alone bought into it all. But none of that mattered anymore. What mattered was the work itself, the act of painting, of expressing, of letting my truth spill onto the canvas without apology.

That shift, learning to embrace fear rather than run from it, changed everything. It showed me that the most powerful work comes from the places we are most afraid to go. Fear, I realized, wasn't an obstacle. It was a guide. A marker pointing directly toward the places I needed to explore, the parts of myself I needed to unearth. And every time I stepped into that space, I found more of myself on the other side.

Even now, as I continue to grow and evolve, I remind myself of that truth. The work is never done. There is always another layer to shed, another story to rewrite, another truth waiting to be uncovered. I know this now: fear will always be there, but it doesn't have to lead. It can walk beside me, a familiar shadow, as I move forward into the light.

*"So have no fear of them, for nothing is covered that will not be revealed, or hidden that will not be known. What I tell you in the dark, say in the light"* -Matthew 10 : 26-27

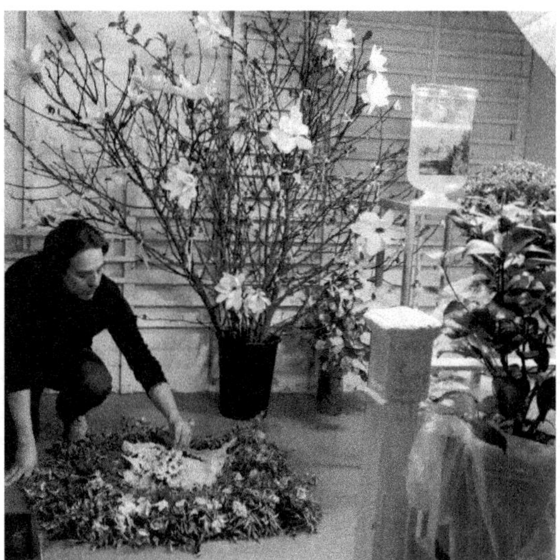

Performance still of 'Self Portrait' from my solo show titled 'Villanueva: Epoch 2020-2023' at Chashama. The floral mandala was created from the fallen debris, a coming to terms with the loss. Photo by me.

## Breaking the Cycle:

It took me decades to realize I needed help to face these inner demons head-on, and with help. Working with a professional opened my eyes to the stories I had been telling myself, stories riddled with red flags planted by my own limiting beliefs. I've always wrestled with self-doubt, questioning whether I'm doing enough, obsessing over the relevance of my work, and, at times, slipping into a victim mentality. But now, when I catch these thoughts creeping in, I work to redirect them, to shift into a more objective perspective.

Of course, this isn't foolproof. Sometimes, I don't notice I'm stuck in a negative loop until I'm in too deep. By then, it takes real effort to untangle myself from the spiral. The truth is, even when life hands me situations that aren't my fault, it's still my choice whether I hold onto the resentment, the fear, the anger. Moving past these feelings isn't easy, but I've learned it is necessary.

One strategy I've been experimenting with is simple and powerful. When I sense negativity creeping in, I cut it off with a firm, "No. We're not doing this right now." Then, I shift gears physically. I make a tangible list of immediate tasks, something I can do at that moment. Giving my hands work to do helps subdue the storm in my head.

But let's be real, sometimes, even that doesn't work. When my mind is in full attack mode, pushing through isn't the answer. In those moments, the best thing I can do is step away, take a walk, breathe deeply, and reset. As we work to break the cycles, we will never win every battle. But we begin to slowly recognize when to fight and when to step back, when to push through, and when to surrender to the moment.

**Relentless Negative Self-Talk:**

Continuing our discussion of negative self-talk, I've also noticed that some of these repetitive thoughts have a way of resurfacing in various forms. They're like persistent salespeople, pitching their negativity from different angles, determined to win me over and prove their opposing viewpoints right. Sometimes, the inner voice is subtle, and other times, downright malicious, depending on the scenario. They thrive on attention and seize any opportunity for a debate. I'm sure I'm not alone in wrestling with these inner voices. This happens when I confront deeply ingrained thoughts or those I struggle to overcome. I know objectively these thoughts are wrong, false, or untrue, yet shaking them takes work.

For instance, recurring thoughts about money or the "starving artist" narrative can quickly lead to a mental spiral. A single delay in payment might ignite a mental frenzy. My therapist calls it "catastrophizing." It's like the mind holding onto old wiring or scars from the days when I had to beg for train fare, or even further back.

The voice in my head starts in: "You're going to go broke, end up homeless."

Even if I remind myself, "The payment will come. It always does."

The voice persists: "Email them again. You're being inconsistent. They're not taking you seriously."

I reply: "They already paid the deposit. Corporate payments take time."

It doubles down: "But rent's due. And the credit card bill. What if it doesn't come through?"

Me: "If it's late, it's late. So be it."

The thoughts ramp up: "What about the landlord's late fee? What will people think if you fall behind?"

And the cycle goes on, thoughts latching and pivoting onto as many insecurities as possible. This is what it is like living with anxiety, and it happens constantly throughout my day. Some days, not even sleep brings solace.

A strategy I've been experimenting with in these extreme cases is to pause and monitor these thoughts. It's like seeing a spoiled child throw a tantrum until they wear themselves out; I've noticed that my thoughts behave in a similar and repetitive way. When they do subside, I can then see where they arise from. If the thoughts surround money, perhaps the fears are about financial insecurities from my youth, growing up poor. I also now realize my intoxicated father is no longer here to escalate the situation, and I am the one, in fact, in control now. Understanding the origins of these traumas is the key to managing the ruminations. I then can step back and say, "There it is again, the frightened inner child who doesn't understand it will be okay, he is loved, and he is safe, now."

So I breathe, observe, let it go, and work MY plan. This is why a subsequent strategy has become keeping a planned, focused, and healthy cash flow in my business practice, which has helped tremendously.

**Stress in the Body:**

Shifting now to how these mental stresses manifest physically. I've come to recognize that stress also leaves its mark on the body. In moments of high anxiety, my heart rate spikes, my breathing becomes shallow, and clarity evaporates. But the longer-term effects are harder to ignore, and in me show up as chronic neck pain, breakouts, hair loss, and brittle nails. Ignoring these warning signs, combined with the relentless chatter of negative self-talk, can eventually spiral into full-blown illness.

Recognizing these patterns in myself has increased my empathy for others. When I see someone caught in their own cycles of self-doubt, I understand that it's not a moment for judgment. I've learned that you can't simply tell someone their thoughts are "wrong"; that only deepens their belief in them. The most effective approach, as I learned through counseling, is to present a different perspective in a neutral manner. However, be aware that it might still be perceived as an attack by someone strongly immersed in their own narrative.

**The Power of Breathing:**

Now, let's explore the simplest yet most effective tool I use to calm negative thoughts: breathing techniques. I understand how cliché this may seem in today's quick-fix self-help culture, but these techniques genuinely help me. They also serve as a stepping stone and bridge to more advanced mindfulness practices, and best of all, they're free for everyone.

Processing emotions takes patience, and more often than not, it dredges up a storm of inner resistance. If I catch myself spiraling, I first acknowledge it because simply noticing is a victory in itself. It used to take me days to realize I was caught in a thought loop, but now I can recognize it in hours, sometimes even minutes.

Once I notice, I breathe.

One of my preferred methods is simple: watching breaths, not counting exactly, just observing. Inhale "1." Exhale "2." "1" & "2", "1" "2", Over and over. The key is <u>not</u> to control the breath but simply observe it. This practice shifts my focus just enough to keep me present, allowing me to return to whatever task is at hand with more clarity.

When I need something more structured, I use box breathing. This method involves inhaling for four counts, holding the breath for four counts, exhaling for four, and then holding again for four. It requires a little more focus, so I don't recommend it while rushing through NYC's midday crowds in the humid summer heat; trust me on that one. But in moments of stillness, this technique can create a tangible shift in my anxiety levels.

**Move Your Body:**

Finally, when my mind is still spiraling, I turn to my body. Physically shaking things up seems to help me, whether it's a brisk walk, a bike ride, or even a few exaggerated stretches. When my brain refuses to let go of a thought, giving it something else to focus on (or, let's be honest, complain about) helps tremendously. Even something as simple as splashing cold water on my face can act as a reset.

Some people swear by yoga, but it's never been my thing. And while traditional meditation works wonders for some, for me, it can sometimes make things worse, trapping me deeper in my thoughts. Instead, I've found my version of mindfulness through my floral practice: cleaning flowers, tidying up, and any repetitive task that allows my hands to take over while my mind quiets.

Whatever the method, the key is this: I don't let a pause become a full stop. Even when I need to step away, I make sure to leave my work at a logical stopping point, again, that little tip I learned years ago from Mrs. Canales. That way, when I return, I can pick up where I left off without feeling like I have to start over.

Fear and self-doubt can be deceptive tricksters. They whisper, they linger, they morph. But we hold the power to meet them head-on. The goal isn't to silence them completely, but to keep going despite them. Progress isn't always linear, but every time we catch ourselves, take a breath, or shift our perspective, we reclaim a little more of our strength. If things get too hard, don't be afraid to reach out for help, and always remember....

As Churchill once said, "If you're going through hell, keep going."

*Disclaimer:* *I'm not a medical professional—these breathing and movement techniques are simply what work for me. If you're dealing with anxiety or health concerns, it's always best to check in with a qualified expert.*

---

## Reflections:

– Have you explored your "artistic shadow"? What have you found there?

– What negative thoughts or inner scripts do you hear most often? Where do you think they arise from?

– What strategies or rituals help you move through them?

# PART III:
## PERSPECTIVE

Breathing in now, from the firmament, we begin to gain perspective. Here, success, scale, and self-worth are reframed through intentional choices and clarity of vision.

# 11

# RESPECT

The phone rang. "This is her. Quiet, I need to concentrate." I whispered to my wife. We were both working out of our home office at the time.

The incoming call was from a party planner whom I'd known for years and was finally reaching out to "start to use me" for her luxury weddings. The promise of weddings with real budgets, enough to finally breathe a bit, was hard to ignore. This, even though deep down I knew I hated doing weddings. It's not that I disliked love or celebration, but I found the performative sameness a bit tiring: the overly scripted timelines, the intense family dynamics, and the Pinterest-perfect aesthetics that often left little space for genuine artistry. But this could really help pay the bills, I thought.

"She is going to want to see good images of your work." She was already halfway through the initial call explaining our upcoming walk-through when I was jolted back to reality. "Oh, yes, yes. I have them right here. I'm emailing them now..." I quickly fumbled around, both with words and with my hands, to grab my external disk drive containing my photos. Then BAM! Off the desk, the drive flew, making a smacking sound against my hardwood floor.

"I...I don't know why the drive won't open. I'll have to get them to you before we meet." I was holding back every shred of wherewithal I could muster because I didn't want to have a panic attack right there over the phone.

That bang should have been my omen, and not some kind of woo-woo, cosmic way, but in the practical, stomach-sinking, Oh-no-you're-disconnected-from-yourself sort of way. I've gotten a lot better over the years at noticing this particularity.

The images were never retrieved. That disk was now a brick. In it, the early floral work, but more importantly, images of my pets as babies. Videos of my dog when we first rescued him from the shelter, his joyous, bouncing play as he realized he'd made it into his new home. All those cherished early memories of that playful pup. Gone. All of it, gone.

The day arrived for the meeting on Long Island, at the typical wedding factory, mock country club venue that I had seen a thousand times by then, freelancing in the Tri-State area. I rented a luxury car for the trip and got myself a new outfit: sports coat, tie, and suede loafers to complete the appearance.

The planner fidgeted nervously beside me, whispering that this client had "another daughter getting married soon." Translation: Don't blow this. As if my attire alone weren't already screaming desperation. She ushered me into the room where the client was impatiently waiting, fiddling with her phone. The client's eyes scanned me up and down. Her clipped tone, as she rattled off the areas that would get flower treatments, said it all. I knew I wasn't getting the job. I felt it. I've always been good that way. It's one of the few benefits of surviving childhood trauma: quickly picking up on silent, unspoken cues, especially when the vibe is *no bueno*.

Head slung down, I entered the car. My wife, who rode out with me as support, said, "That was quick. How'd it go?" I quickly retorted, "Ugh. I just want to get home, get out of these clothes, and take a shower. I feel icky."

"What do you mean?" She said. I never answered. I didn't have the energy to answer, so we rode back to the city in silence.

## The Hangover of Pretending:

The nuances of respect are often hidden behind a wall of subtleties and occasionally insecurities. In this chapter, we'll explore just that. Delving into what it means in our work, what it reveals about us as creatives, and how it shapes the way we engage with others. At its core, it's about recognizing that the way we show up in the world is the clearest expression of self-respect.

I often think about that drive home. How quiet it was, because I was still afraid to confront those feelings out loud, even with someone I trusted. I'd pursued that job, even though it never felt right in my body. I wore that opportunity like a polished costume, agreeable, professional, but altogether fake. And the weight of that disconnection landed, just like the drive, with a hard and brutal thump.

This wasn't about the planner or the client. It was about me. It was about the ways I'd contorted myself toward someone else's version of success. I'd overruled my own instincts in the name of ambition, and my nervous system finally called it. The clients' and the planners' needs and expectations were completely valid, even if my own needs were misaligned; this is of critical importance to acknowledge and account for.

The crash of that external hard drive hitting the floor was the alarm signal, or at least it should have been. It wasn't mystical. It wasn't fate. It was just my nervous system screaming, "Something is off here!" Since then, I've learned to listen to that kind of siren.

It was one of the first, truly accountable moments when I felt genuine anger with myself for being dishonest about who I am.

This wasn't the first time I'd stretched myself thin, straining to look like I belonged, or felt the unnamed anger that goes along with it. It also wasn't the last.

There were too many times to count that I agreed to a high-profile launch party or event that wanted "something edgy" but really meant expensive for me and budget for them. Or the interior design client who said they wanted my aesthetic, then slowly chipped away at it until it looked like their own work. What they were really looking for was someone to execute, quietly. And I kept thinking I could somehow will it into a partnership.

I eventually started to notice a pattern that every time I said yes when my gut was screaming "No!" I came home needing to wash it off, to get rid of that ick. Ultimately, what I've learned is that there is a subtle yet powerful difference between a client deciding to "use me" and having them choose our services. This shift in perspective has allowed for an understanding that both honors the client's needs and their right to express them, while giving me permission to stay true to the values that guide mine.

**Drawing the Line:**

By treating myself with kindness and respect, I set the standard for how others should treat me. A wise client once shared this with me, and it has stuck with me ever since.

Now, one of my go-to phrases with potential clients, vendors, or collaborators is: "If I can help you, I will. But sometimes, I may not be the right fit." It's a healthy mindset to accept that it's truly no one's fault if it does not work out. Sometimes, we are not on the same path. Respect is standing firm in those boundaries. The challenge then becomes letting go of relationships that are not aligned quickly, and doing so without, or at least with little, resentment or bitterness. Honestly, this is still a tough one, no matter how you frame it.

As a business owner, I interact with many people, most of whom are wonderful, collaborative, and motivated to create something great. But occasionally, the opposite is true. As much as I dislike it, I've had to 'fire' clients and discontinue using vendors and subcontractors when our values didn't align or when I felt disrespected or undervalued. It doesn't happen often, but when it does, I trust my instincts.

One situation I still think about involved a long-time vendor who would misplace my orders and unexpectedly jack up the prices of the goods. This often left me scrambling to find replacements at the last minute, which affected not just me, but also my team and clients. Despite multiple conversations, nothing changed. Eventually, I had to step away and find other alternatives. It wasn't easy, but I had to choose the long-term health of my work over the ease of staying agreeable.

In full transparency, I've also been the one fired by garden clients before. They told me, "We don't need an artist. We just need someone to show up, clean up, and replace whatever dies with simple flowering plants." And honestly, they were right, I wasn't the right fit. I can't do that kind of work: just show up, keep my mouth shut, clean and replace without offering feedback or opinions. That's just not me.

**Respecting Your Rates and the Red Flags:**

I wish I'd been more grounded in self-respect during those early years. People-pleasing kept me from saying "no" to clients, and I often paid the price, both financially and emotionally.

For a long time, I did the financial shuffle: undercharging, over-delivering, then silently resenting it when things went sideways. But I wasn't angry at the client. I was frustrated with myself.

I told myself those budget jobs would lead to bigger, better ones. The ones that paid well, brought exposure, or opened doors.

But let me be clear: that nearly never happens. I'll repeat that, because it took me years to believe it myself. <u>That almost never happens.</u>

When a project doesn't generate profit, there's no magical backup fund to pull from when things go awry. You end up covering the gap from your own pocket, time, money, and energy. I had a mentor who warned me about this early on, but I wasn't ready to hear it. I thought every yes was progress.

As a result, I found myself constantly 'busy,' often wearing this deceptive badge of honor, yet not making any real progress.

> **Side Note:** *I'm working on removing the word 'busy' from overuse in my vocabulary as well; it is a catchphrase that floral designers cling to in the height of event season. But all too often, it is part bragging right and part a cry for help as burnout pushes the edges...and says nothing about authentic progress.*

I was using the next job to pay for the last, spinning in circles, exhausted. It felt like I was running on a treadmill with a dollar bill dangling just out of reach. Sadly, I was the only one who built that treadmill, and getting off of it took a lot of painful lessons.

Over time, I've learned to spot certain red flags in potential clients, patterns I now recognize more quickly:

### The Budget Peddler

This one pitches small-budget projects with the promise of bigger things down the line: "I'm here to help you grow!" But when you raise your rates, they vanish, off to find someone cheaper. Bonus clue: tasks sneak in under a breezy "Can you just add..."

### The Carrot Dangler

Closely related, this one always has a hypothetical future gig: "My friend owns a restaurant and is looking for a florist," or "This will be great exposure, my cousin works in PR." I've learned to smile and redirect by saying, "That sounds great, but let's stay focused on the project at hand."

### The Last-Minute Designer

These clients may have the budget and the vision. However, they often come in hot with a project that requires more time and trust than the timeline allows. This is a big red flag, especially if I haven't worked with them before. Just know, if someone brings fire to your doorstep and calls it collaboration, it's not.

## The Friend of a Friend

Even referrals from great clients aren't always aligned with my process or offerings. These days, I take on new clients only after proper vetting, even if they come highly recommended. Respecting your own standards protects everyone involved.

> ***Pro Tip:*** *Small-budget events often require the same amount of time and labor as larger ones. The difference is that with no room for support, you end up absorbing the cost. There's a reason the phrase "being cheap is expensive" keeps showing up in creative business. A colleague taught me this one, and I see the truth in it constantly.*

I want to be clear, I'm grateful for my clients and the work I get to do. This is grounded in finding clarity, not cynicism. These stories come from hard-won experience. And while some situations stem from mismatched values, not malice, it's still my job to draw the line.

Holding these boundaries means saying no to opportunities that once felt essential. And I remember what that's like, when every job feels like a lifeline, when there's no fallback plan, no savings, no cushion. Just the will to keep going.

Once I committed to valuing my work, the shift happened, and my circumstances started to reflect that. I raised my rates. I stopped cushioning every quote with "extras" to justify the price. I began communicating my value clearly and without apology.

And to my surprise? The right clients didn't hesitate.

They simply said, "Great. When can we start?"

Turns out, the only people who flinched at my worth were the ones hoping I won't name it.

## Ballrooms and Galleries:

I think this is a good enough spot to talk about two very different rooms I've encountered in my career, ballrooms and galleries.

In the ballroom, the hotel lobby, the crystal palaces, eyes go down. You're sweaty, hauling buckets, your back aching from schlepping boxes. The Help mutters, "Don't leave a mess."

In the gallery, eyes lift. You're the artist. People ask where to place things. They watch their step. They ask, "Is there anything else you need?"

Same flowers. Same hands. Very different gaze.

This is the playing field of the creative life. It can be brutal. It can be beautiful. And it's where the real work happens. So, should you choose it? That's a question only you can answer. It offers wealth, validation, competition, connection, and all the opposites that come with it. Most of which rarely make it to the highlight reels.

That's why I teach the way I do, honestly, fully. Because when someone says, "Oh, I want to do this," I remember what it felt like to start from zero. I know how hard it is to build momentum, to stack small wins until they matter. I know how this work tests you. It weeds out hobbyists. It humbles egos. It asks everything. And the rewards, it gives sparingly, but when it does, it's gold.

So when I'm asked, "Aren't you worried about people copying your ideas?" my answer is always the same: No.

If someone wants to step into this arena, I welcome them. Because I know who I am, what I am made of, and what it has taken to stay.

If I can help, even just with a warm *bravo*, I will. Because this craft was never built on secrecy, it was built on shared knowledge. Florists helping florists.

**This Is Also Self-Respect:**

Since we're staying real, it also has to be said that some people will just flat-out diminish you. No matter how generous, talented, or sincere you are, there will be those who dismiss your creative abilities, question your value, or treat your work like it's theirs or disposable. Sometimes it's envy, sometimes projection, sometimes just plain ignorance. But whatever the root, their behavior doesn't define your worth.

Learning to hold your brilliance unapologetically, especially if you come from a lineage of people-pleasers, service workers, or "don't rock the boat" survivors, can be its own rite of passage. I come from generations of people trained not to upset the boss. To smile through it, as mentioned in the chapter about Intention. To be grateful even while being overlooked or talked down to.

And in certain spaces, ones where art is a given, where creating is assumed to be a choice, not a self-built life, it became clear to me just how stark the divide really was. Some people were raised to believe their voice mattered. Others were raised to be useful. I didn't know that was even a distinction until I found myself in rooms where status was assumed and the struggle was <u>optional</u>, where I was both invisible and expected to perform.

But the truth is: your work has value, even when others can't see it.

You don't have to earn the right to take up space.

Respecting yourself as a creative means reclaiming authority over your voice, vision, and time.

**Sometimes the most radical act is simply not explaining yourself, not staying small, and not asking for permission.**

It takes practice and nerve, but this is self-respect in a creative life.

**Standing Firm:**

As you can see, sometimes respect means telling the full story, the parts where it hurts, where it's hard, where you wonder if it's even worth it. Because let's be real: if you don't already feel the heart-swelling wonder of this work, the immense joy of being constantly surrounded by beauty, and if the thought of not doing it feels as counterintuitive as ceasing to breathe, then maybe this life isn't for you.

**You shouldn't need me to define this love for you. You'll already know if it's inside you. This life will take everything you've got. We give it anyway because of that love.**

There are other paths. Gentler ones. Ones that don't demand every ounce of your being just to make a living from beauty. And there's nothing wrong with choosing them.

But if you're still here, if something in you lights up even now, then maybe, just maybe, you've found your place.

So, then what's the reward in all this? When you stand firm in your values, the work begins to meet you in a different way. You slowly begin to feel at home in your skin. I'm finally at a point where I can walk into a meeting dressed in a simple linen skirt and my work boots, knowing that the right people will show up in my life. The right clients return, not because of the performance, but because of the work. They ask first, "Are you available?" without first assuming I am. The tension softens. You get introduced with honor, "This is Juan. He has great taste...you're in good hands." Full stop.

Now, I've made room to create freely without shrinking and collaborate without resentment. I sense the shift rooted in my body. It shows up in how I enter and exit spaces. I am no longer seeking external validation, as I am deeply anchored in self-respect. The focus is now on alignment, embracing my authority and confidently exploring the intricacies of my creative process, including its beauty, all the messiness, and everything in between.

How we show up in our work is an act of self-respect. It extends to our clients, our families, and ultimately, to how we live. At the heart of it all is a deep reverence for ourselves and for the vision that fuels our work.

As creatives, our purpose is to share, to move, to inspire, in whatever form that takes. A great piece of art really can change someone's life. That is a powerful truth, one worth honoring and honing. Those with the ability to create have a responsibility to contribute. Each of us carries a unique perspective on the world and our place in it. In expressing that, we respect our craft and honor life itself.

And when the world tries to hold you down, when your work is dismissed or disrespected, self-respect is what keeps your hands and voice steady. It is the solid ground you can stand firm on.

## Reflections:

– How has respect or the lack of it shaped your creative practice?

– What red flags have surfaced in your journey, and how have you responded with boundaries?

– Does this creative pursuit still resonate with you, in both its glory and its trials?

# 12

# BUILDING MOMENTUM

The season roared in, with the all-too-familiar rush of wholesalers, boutique buyers, and florals flooding the Javits Center's 3 million-plus square feet, in a frenetic high fashion marketplace that surges with life biannually. My crew and I wove floral art throughout its sprawling halls and booths. Along the way, filling last-minute requests and dodging egos as sharp as thorns. "Not a problem, will do." I'd say. It's the mantra of the season. Eyes low, voice steady, to the union crew: "Whenever you can." Over the years, I've learned to move through it gently, not always with grace, but with enough grit to stay upright, and still get the job done with some dignity intact.

I won't dress it up; pulling that season's market off with ten days' notice was creating its own kind of magic. And still, I made it happen.

The morning after the installation, I was back just before sunrise. A few steps from the door, I took a deep breath and looked up at the starry sky overhead. The seagulls, fluttering about and welcoming the new day, sang their judgmental song. There it was again: that old, familiar feeling of loss, heartache, and bewilderment. I hadn't arrived there that morning because it was on the schedule or part of the billable hours. I was simply still tethered to the event. I wanted to deadhead what needed it, scan for florals that might blow out before the three-day mark, and find some kind of closure.

My body was beat down in that deep, bone-aching way, the kind you stop complaining about because it never leaves. I hadn't really slept. Hadn't properly documented the work either, so I used that bleary-eyed walk-through for a few quick photos, chasing the good light in the empty halls. The silence in those early hours is healing, I've found. It didn't look as bad as I'd remembered leaving it. The client was right; it was beautifully executed.

It's funny how exhaustion distorts your vision, causing you to perceive failure where none exists.

There were other jobs tucked between, a couple of NY Bridal Week installs, before a three-day teaching intensive in Monterrey, Mexico, already on the books. My mother was frantic about it; she had already been in that state for several weeks, disturbed by stories of the cartel and late-night news clips. She told me she had lit some *velas* in her flower shop. "It rivaled the cathedral!" my sister later told me.

"*¡No salgas del hotel! No vayas a ninguna parte donde no debas estar... y llámame, diario.*" My mother begged..."Okay *Amá*! Yes, I'll call you daily, and won't leave the hotel at all! Please relax, I'm in more than good hands." I replied.

But that class, that I taught, entirely in Spanish for the first time, was medicine for me. The rhythm of it, the steady hands, the way tradition held its ground while I nudged it forward. Testing edges. Learning their ways, showing mine. And despite sceptical eyes that lingered throughout the process, the work landed.

I half-joked with my host that when I got back to the city, I'd be making a floral mannequin for the first time. A floral sculpture that needed to last ten days in all fresh flowers, and still had no idea what I'd be making,

"But I know it'll be great!" I told her, half-smirking, as a bead of sweat made its way down my forehead.

That upcoming project was going to be in the newly developed Hudson Yards. And like most things that sound harmless when you initially say yes, it became a trial that stretched everything I thought I knew. Mechanics pushed to their limits. Late nights turned to predawn mornings, a gallon of tears shed in between, and in it all, I had a team that showed up when it counted. We took home 'Best in Show,' but the real prize was what we built: trust in each other. A different kind of currency.

The check wasn't much. It never is, in those kinds of projects. But as I've always said, "You have to go into those projects knowing they don't pay much and no real work will come from them." Some work is simply about the fight it takes to get them made. About the bruises and bone-tired nights, yet you keep going because *"No hay otra"*, there's no other way "we have to work", and there's always another job waiting, that needs doing. These projects are meant to teach us what we're made of when no one's watching, and how to keep going anyway. The writing of this book has been no different.

Taking another deep breath, barely.

Gala season rolled in next, fast and hard, and the calendar pushed quickly toward the end of 2019. And somewhere in there, in one of those solitary elevator rides, picking rose thorns out of my hands, or a late-night cab ride back to the studio, buckets and bags stacked on top of my laps, I remember thinking: this is it. That season of stacked projects built on momentum had been a patchwork of peaks and valleys. It was a mix of beauty and a balance that ran the razor's edge of burnout. And something deep in me felt the next season would be the one to tear the map clean.

**Layering:**

There's a strange ache that comes at the end of a creative project. Relief, yes, but also a kind of stillness that can feel like loss. Like deadheading the last petal from a bloom you've been tending for weeks in a garden.

There's pride in what's been made, but also a space that echoes with the question: Now what?

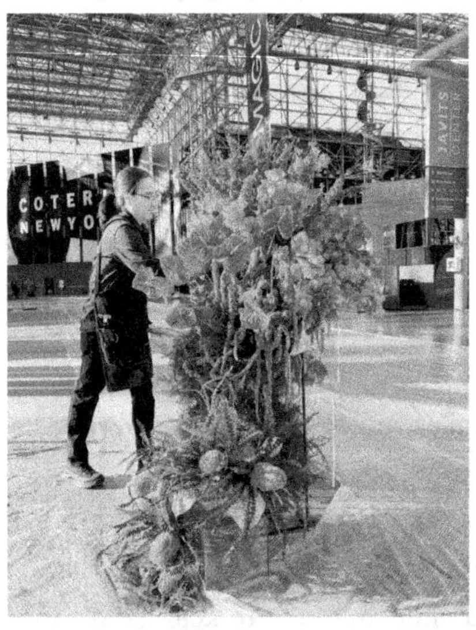

Putting finishing touches on a floral sculpture at the Javits Center in New York City, in 2024. Photo by T.S. Flores.

In this chapter, we'll explore how layering our creative efforts can build stamina and deepen our capacity for surprise. When you approach it with intention, this method keeps your life moving forward. It creates a way to hold ourselves up through the inevitable lows, while staying open to what's next, building momentum in careers and lives.

What I've learned is that momentum doesn't have to end when a project does. In fact, I've come to rely on the power of overlapping projects. Allowing one project to push the next into motion before the first one even finishes. It's the creative version of leaving a thread untied, just long enough to catch the loop of what's coming.

This rhythm of compounding projects is the catalyst for how I work now. But don't confuse this with overcommitting or overproducing. It is more in line with keeping the energy moving forward, so the silence after completion doesn't consume me entirely. Using a garden metaphor again, if done well, the garden always has something blooming, always has something going to seed, and always has a new shoot emerging, before the invariable rest.

**Feeling Ghosted:**

I first learned the importance of overlapping projects as a freelance florist. When working on events, we would spend several days prepping hard goods, receiving and conditioning flowers, and creating centerpieces and arrangements. On the event day, we would install everything and then be sent home before seeing the project finished or hearing if the clients liked it. This left me with an unsettled feeling and unanswered questions. It felt like the events and people I'd been working with for over a week would suddenly ghost me. Later, while running my own business, I began noticing that this feeling would come up again and again after completing big projects. This happened even as I saw projects through to the end, and was praised for a job well done.

What was this feeling, and why was I continuing to experience it? I liken it to a hangover, but mentally and emotionally. Working on large-scale projects can take months of development and require tons of physical and mental energy. It's after completing those projects that the next day, I've often felt like I had been in a physical fight and gotten whipped. It can seem as if, suddenly, the creation is born one day, and then poof! It's gone, sent out into the world, never heard from again. This has left me sitting there afterward investigating, obsessing...So, what's next? This is when the seeds of rumination are planted in my mind.

The feeling of loss is pronounced and familiar. When I lost my dog, one of the most complex parts was getting over his scheduled walks. For the first few weeks, every time our usually scheduled walks would come up, I'd once again be enveloped with the realization and grief, knowing he was not there. This still tugs on my heartstrings. These routines that our bodies get used to can get hardwired into our psyche and can be painfully difficult to ignore.

Working on multiple projects has helped me discover a way to ease this lingering discomfort. It brings to mind the people who decide to adopt a puppy when their older dog starts to show its age. I used to think to myself, "I could never do that," as I watched my beloved dog grow older. Seeing other people walking a playful, energetic puppy alongside their older canine didn't resonate with me. But as I write this chapter, I'm starting to appreciate the emotional depth behind that choice.

**Keep on Creating:**

So, besides dealing with this sense of loss, what are some other benefits of overlapping projects? The beauty of compounding projects lies in their ability to propel me forward, building momentum. I've made it a personal practice of challenging myself to keep my creative engine running, but staying mindful that it is not about competing with others. This practice helps me combat occasional dips in motivation and avoid complacency while sticking to my core values.

I've experienced many seasons that resonate like the one in the story in the intro of this chapter. So many, in fact, that they begin to blur into one, at times. And I have to check in on my Instagram feed for the correct timeline of how it's all unfolded.

Stacking projects doesn't leave time to obsess over the last completed one. It's my way of slow detachment from the outcome of the creations. Even if at times it straddles repression. Also, I often find that in the midst of doing, I must create something entirely different after concentrating so heavily on one job. This works for my mind. You see, this method of stacking projects allows for the creation to flow through me. I'll reiterate this point: When this is working well, I am not forcing the overlapping projects but allowing one project to flow into the next.

Occasionally, I do find myself out of alignment, competing with others in my industry to outproduce. This typically occurs when I start accepting large-scale installations or events that lack artistic interest and are merely viewed as a paycheck. While earning money is not inherently evil, I've noticed that I can quickly lose sight of my original purpose when indiscriminately accepting every project. A few telling signs this is happening are that I almost invariably feel overwhelming stress, frustration, impatience, and attachment to the work's outcome while simultaneously experiencing emotional and physical fatigue.

**Getting Started with Compounding Projects:**

It's one thing to talk about momentum when you're already in motion. But in the beginning, it can feel impossible to see the next step, let alone a string of them. I remember those stretches clearly, when I was running on fumes, chasing jobs that barely paid, saying yes to things I didn't know how to do yet, just to stay moving. And if you're in that place now, I get it.

There's no perfect map for how to build momentum, but here are a few things I've learned along the way:

**<u>Start where you are.</u>**

Resources will almost always feel limited at the start, whether it's money, connections, experience, or time. But that doesn't mean you're stuck. Some of the smartest, sharpest solutions I've ever seen came from people working with scraps. What matters is learning to work with what's in front of you. Say yes to what you can manage, be honest about what you can't, and keep showing up.

**<u>Let one thing lead to the next.</u>**

You don't have to take on everything at once. Balance matters, even if it's imperfect. The key is to pay attention to the connections between projects. That small commission you took might teach you something you'll need for the next one. A chance conversation could open a door a year from now. Don't treat every job like a solo act. When I started, I was constantly looking for where the overlap could happen, where one could inform or build toward another. That's how momentum builds naturally, without burning you out.

### Hold on to your why.

When the calendar fills up and you're chasing deadlines, it's easy to disconnect from the reason you started. I've been there too. Overcommitting and running on autopilot often caused me to lose sight of the true meaning of my work. It's important to pause and check in with yourself. Ask if this project, or this season, is still aligned with the bigger picture you're building (again, back to those core building chapters earlier in this book). Doing is important, but it should stay connected to the deeper reasons you started creating in the first place.

### Stay Visible.

And if nothing else, stay visible. Share your work. Reach out to people. Say yes to opportunities you feel good about, even if they're small or imperfect. Look for resonance, for what gives you those goosebumps or makes your heart flutter…those are the tells. In the early days, every experience is a chance to learn, to meet someone, to practice, to build confidence. Little by little, the next step reveals itself. Until one day, while scrolling through thousands of photos, you hit one, and the flood of memories comes back, "Oh, crap, I forgot all about that, that was a really cool project!"

### *No Hay De Otra:*

A friend from art school, who came from a different world entirely, once said, in a rare moment of honesty, "What surprises and inspires me most is that you never give up."

At the time, I laughed it off, assuming he meant I was always hustling because I had no other choice.

But looking back, I think he may have seen something I didn't yet understand about myself, that my refusal to stop was my way of building momentum. It was discipline and purpose that I clung to, the threads tied to my roots, that softly resonate in code, saying, "You don't have the luxury to fail."

These days, occasionally, people ask me about my greatest accomplishment. It's a question that always gives me pause, because there isn't just one. How do you pick a single moment that defines the whole, when each season, each risk, each moment of grit has mattered?

What I'm proudest of is that I never stopped. Even when I was burned out, overlooked, or doubting myself, I just kept creating and evolving. That stubborn refusal to give up or give in was the real win.

Growing up, my family used to tease me:

"*Mira tú,* you're never satisfied. *¿Qué te falta, hombre?* What else do you need?"

It stuck. That critique landed somewhere between being slightly misunderstood and a hard truth.

They weren't completely wrong. I've always had this fire. Not dissatisfaction, exactly...something more akin to drive. A hunger that refuses to die.

And now, looking back, I can see it clearly: Chasing momentum isn't something you outgrow. It becomes the engine. It's what's carried me through the low seasons, the quiet days, the setbacks, and surprises.

It's what builds the body of work and the life.

So maybe that's my answer. My greatest accomplishment is my ongoing refusal to stop moving, because *no hay de otra.*

## The Unexpected Gift of Documentation:

And if there's another reward worth noting, beyond accolades or recognition, it's this: documentation. One unexpected benefit of overlapping creative projects is that you end up with a ton of viable content, as a natural byproduct of the work. Every sketch, installation, failed attempt, or behind-the-scenes moment becomes part of the ongoing story.

I've started to treat documentation as a form of grounding. Sharing my work, even the bumpy pieces, helps me stay connected to the process. Not the performance, necessarily, but the nuts and bolts of it. Especially in the fine arts, where the work can be more abstract and harder to explain, it's been freeing to post "bad" art or unfinished thoughts. With this,

I've started adding a mantra to this practice: "No one's really paying that much attention anyway."

Don't get me wrong, I'm not diminishing my work. I'm releasing the ego from obsessing over its reaction to it. The truth is, most people are overstimulated, just doing their best to keep up with their own lives. And that includes me.

I've had conversations with my wife where I'll say, "My newest piece? What do you mean? It's done and you already 'liked' it on Instagram," and we'll both laugh. She's done the same to me. These are the moments that remind me: visibility doesn't always equal presence. And silence isn't the same as rejection.

This change in perspective has enabled me to remain receptive and unencumbered while continuing to create with purpose. Not every project will go viral, and not every work will resonate. However, that has never been the aim.

The essence lies in the act of doing. The act of showing up and documenting. No, not for the algorithm, but for the sake of recording our evolving identity. And no, not everything needs to be shared. Nor does every season demand output. I'm infamous for stepping away from posting sometimes, because the impulse to document can sneakily become just another performance. I've learned (and relearned) to check in with myself and question, "Am I capturing this moment for insight, or just avoiding stillness?"

Maybe that's the real takeaway here: momentum isn't a race or a performance. It's a quiet, yet faithful unfolding of the creative spirit, shaping character as we build our careers.

Stay focused there. Document that.

Learning to ride the waves of overlapping projects has saved me more times than I can count. It softens the crash that follows a big push, and it calms the ache of the anticlimax. It centers my being as I wait and watch the next set slowly rolling in, long after the applause has quieted. When you keep paddling, not frantically but faithfully, you learn how to surf the waves of your career. And in the end, you'll find some days are swells, some are choppy soup bowls, and some are simply flat, and that is also what it is all about.

Building momentum teaches you that not every arrangement or project will be noticed, nor will every effort be praised. And still, you show up. Hands blistered, heart open, faith intact. If you're aligned, you might find yourself there as a sign of your ongoing growth in the work, not because the ego demands it.

But don't forget to take a pause. The doing alone will drain you. Without rest, reflection, and a return to center, momentum turns reckless. The real challenge is knowing when to lean in and paddle your hardest to land that wave, and when to lean back as you wait for the next set. If you're listening, your body, your spirit, and yes, your flowers will tell you.

So keep going. Keep resting. Keep making.

The art, this life, will find you in both motion and stillness.

---

## Reflections:

– What role do compounding projects play in your momentum?

– How do you celebrate your wins, big or small?

– How do you recognize when rest is needed, and how do you make space for it?

# 13

## DEFINING SUCCESS

A few days ago, I dropped off my weekly flowers and then went back to the studio to work on a new painting, a large one, 53 inches square, in a medium I hadn't touched in twenty years: oil paints. That smell of the paint now lingers in the studio like the scent of a returned love. The subject of the painting is "The Moon" from the Major Arcana. And it's fitting since the studio's on lockdown again, as I search for clarity. Outside, the air hums with a strange, 2020-like tension. Same quiet. Less dread and much more focus on unveiling the truth lurking beneath it all.

As I write this, I am waiting for gardening reply emails to come through. Keeping the plates spinning: flowers, paint, words, soil. Not always perfect, but it's been working.

Still, tending the seed of an idea that started years ago, with a voice in my head screaming, "I should write about this bullshit." Later, it was students who pressed, "Why don't you have a book?" Eventually, this writing project has caught its own pulse. A life that has required its own steady nurturing.

And the question remains, is this just a field report? An artsy florist manual? Maybe. Or maybe it's just a more open space to say what can't be said on social media. Dialogue for anyone building a life without a blueprint or the funds to take the class. A tangible record. Evidence of a working artist in this city, in this decade.

The flowers are still here.

I'm still breaking old rules, making new ones. Still chasing those rare moments when it all comes together, when the brush moves right, when the stems balance nicely, when the words land clean.

To hell with status. The milestone now is alignment.

I'm still not represented. Not platformed. Not traditionally published. But I'm working. I'm living. Holding it all down: this artist's life, with paint, flowers, plants, words, and a heapful of faith.

So what has the work become? Me…a stronger, purer version. The skills I've gained, the bruises I've endured, the lessons I've learned, and the questions I continue to ask. A why that keeps shifting but stays mine.

I am completely sober now. Living the life I once only dreamed of. Fear still accompanies me, yes, but my faith has grown stronger than my fear. It's the proof that lives in the work…for those who are willing to see it. And, I suppose that is what my success looks like. But what is success anyway?

**Perspective:**

How do we define success? When have we outgrown our place? And what should we consider when the time comes to scale?

In this final chapter of the main narrative, we'll explore these questions. And like much of what we've covered, I think you'll find that success isn't so easily pinned down either. It's rarely black and white, and much more often a matter of perspective. Because for many of us, especially those creating from a place of integrity, success can't simply be measured by the size of our ventures or the almighty dollar.

My creative process has always been value-driven, rooted in a pursuit of service. That's why, throughout this book, I've returned again and again to core beliefs. They're the keystones, the internal architecture that holds everything else up. Without them, I couldn't define the values that guide my business practices.

For me, success looks like being present with every project I touch. To someone else, this might sound exhausting or inefficient, and that's fine. We each have to determine what matters most to us, so we can then clearly define success in our own words.

This brings to mind a moment that brought this idea into sharp focus. In a business class I took through the City of New York, the instructor asked a simple but potent question:

"What does success look like to you, and how can it tangibly be defined?"

At the time, I had been running my business for five or six years, yet I had never seriously considered that question. My immediate response was, "Well, success must be about continuous expansion and making a lot of money." But that wasn't a well-intentioned answer; it lacked specificity.

Our instructor shared his own definition: he wanted a team in place so he could work remotely from anywhere in the world while his staff handled the day-to-day operations. He also wanted to take a three-week vacation with his family every year. Not bad goals.

At that moment, I realized I had never taken a real vacation since starting my business, either. My version of success was simple: I wanted to be able to step away for three to five days, just a short break away from the city. That became my new benchmark.

Over time, my definition of success has evolved. Yes, vacation is still an important marker, but I've added others:
- Having leisure time at home or with my wife
- Being able to shop for myself, my family, or my business without worrying about every dime

- Not needing to check my bank account obsessively before making a larger purchase
- Feeling secure in my finances, with a backup nest egg and a growing 401(k)
- Devoting time to what I love, reducing stress, and prioritizing my physical and mental health
- Contributing with my art and my teaching, as I honor and inspire others to do the same
- Treating myself, friends, or family to a meal whenever possible

These don't have to be extravagant, sweeping achievements. Some of the simplest aspects of life are the most valuable.

I've lived through times when financial stability wasn't my reality, when Sunday dinner meant another bowl of ramen noodles. That contrast has shaped my perspective. Today, success means being able to make choices that align with my ever-evolving needs and aspirations. The real key here is that I've learned no one else can define success for me; I must continually decide what feels right for my own life.

**To Scale:**

But defining success is only the beginning. Once we start to experience even a glimpse of it, however personal or modest, it opens the door to a more complex question: Is it time to scale?

That question has been a recurring theme in my own journey, especially as new opportunities arise. Do I maintain what I've built? Or is it time to scale? Is expansion an accurate signal of growth, or just the next rung on someone else's ladder?

These aren't theoretical questions. They come with real trade-offs, and answering them requires as much honesty as any creative act. I often get asked by students when they will know it's the right time to grow or expand a creative business. The truth is, I still ask myself the same thing, and again, it often starts with a checklist. Questions I considered could be:

1) Am I prepared for extended work hours?

2) Will I be okay with the time required away from my family?

3) Am I okay holding onto debt? Good debt, that is.

4) How will being unable to do as many hands-on artistic projects affect me in the long term?

5) Do I want to pivot from 'making' the work to primarily managing people?

6) Can I manage the unending pressure of 'putting out fires' that will arise?

7) Will I accept the responsibilities of maintaining enough business to support the additional staff required?

8) Do I have the mental fortitude to handle all the additional pressures (and anxiety) to expand the business?

9) What is holding me back? Is it fear (of success or failure)?

10) Will the added income, the MONEY, be worth the sacrifices and adjustments listed above?

And yes, I get it, some of these are indeed reflections of internalized fear. But as I've learned in my welding & carpentry practice, having a healthy dose of fear, especially when working with 'power tools', can be helpful.

**A Dream to Expand:**

In the growth of my own business, I've felt the push to expand several times. One of the main obstacles in the floral industry is its inherent seasonality, and it's also incredibly cyclical. While that could seem like a negative, it's actually helped me carve out my little niche. When other bridal-focused companies are swamped with weddings, I might not be fully booked, and vice versa.

Diversifying my business has carried me through some of the "hard" times. The changing seasons have pushed me into unexpected projects, which, in turn, have helped me grow. It really only starts to feel hectic when those larger projects begin to overlap. That's when I test the true capacity of my micro-business.

In February 2020, I was swamped with work and heading into a banner year. I was on track to finally hit a financial milestone I'd been chasing for years. My projects were getting larger, and fulfilling orders out of my tiny studio space was becoming increasingly complicated.

Around that time, a neighbor in my building, who had had his unit for over a decade, announced he was downsizing. I started dreaming. The rent would be tight, but I envisioned the possibilities. I was pivoting back into painting and could see a setup. I planned to divide the space into thirds. At the far end was a twelve-foot-wide by fifteen-foot-tall wall, ideal for painting. I imagined using a pipe and drape for privacy during floral productions. In the center would be work tables. Up front, I planned to install a bandsaw for custom projects and considered hiring part-time help for the studio and garden clients.

It was still more of a dream than a plan.

When the pandemic hit, like many, I assumed the lockdown would be brief. But as we all know, what followed was months of uncertainty. The future grew murkier. Just months earlier, I was on track for my best financial year. And, yes, even that early in the year, I could project this (another reason to keep track of and know your financials year to year). Then suddenly, I couldn't tell what I'd be returning to or if I'd be returning at all.

When I did make it back to my tiny studio, I began clearing it out. I was sure I'd lose the space, so I prepared to move my gardening equipment into storage. My plan was simple: run my "essential services" gardening business from that unit. Then something unexpected happened. The tenants negotiated a discounted rate with the landlords during the lockdowns. That cooperation saved me. Since my studio was already small and affordable, I was able to stay. I cannot overstate the relief that brought. It was a profoundly humbling experience.

The pandemic forced me to pause and reflect on what all this momentum was leading to and why. Was I building toward something I truly wanted? Or something I had assumed was required of me?

**Root Pruning:**

In bonsai, when a plant becomes root-bound and outgrows its container, one option is to upsize the planter. The other approach is root pruning. By trimming the roots and keeping the plant in the same pot, you allow it to thrive within its existing space. The plant will be sensitive and vulnerable for a while, but ultimately, it will bounce back, stronger and more contained.

The same principle applies to business. Growth isn't always about expansion. Sometimes, it's about refining, reshaping, and maintaining what already works. As an entrepreneur, I've come to realize that I don't have to scale endlessly. I decide what kind of business I run, fully aware that I alone bear the consequences of my risks, both the wins and the failures.

I've come to accept that having a micro-business is more than okay when it's done intentionally. There is no one-size-fits-all definition of success, and I don't have to follow the conventional commercial model of perpetual growth to have a thriving venture. It all comes down to the values I set for my company.

Early in the book, I wrote about the importance of starting where you are, building within the boundaries of your current resources, rather than rushing to expand. That idea circles back here. Staying small by choice isn't about playing it safe or holding onto limiting beliefs. It's a grounded decision. As our careers evolve, it becomes easy to confuse expansion with progress, especially in creative work, where it can seem like more space equals more success. But sometimes, what we actually need is better systems, not bigger rooms.

I've seen it play out over time, especially in the transient flow of designers through our building. Not every move leads to growth. Any experienced container gardener will confirm that the same applies to plants. Moving a plant to a larger pot too early or too dramatically can hinder its growth and overall health.

So please consider that every investment, especially one as significant as upsizing a studio, must earn its place. It should unlock new potential, amplify returns, or elevate performance. If it doesn't, we owe it to the work to pause, reassess, and redirect resources toward what truly matters.

**Staying Small is Okay:**

This realization was reaffirmed while watching an old episode of Shark Tank. One of the investors made an observation that stuck with me. They acknowledged that while the entrepreneur pitching had built a great small business, there would be little room to scale the business. Then they added, "And that's okay. Not all businesses are meant to be big." This landed hard, and I instantly thought, "Exactly!"

Why should every business strive to become a big-box store? Success isn't one-size-fits-all. For me, success means serving my clients, bringing beauty into their lives, leaving space in my schedule to service their incoming needs as needed, and making a living while doing what I love. There is deep honor in that, in contributing to my community in a way that feels meaningful, sustainable, and true to who I am.

And perhaps most importantly, in protecting the space I need to keep creating, not just producing.

**Ask and Receive:**

Before expanding your business, do your research. Make your own list of perceived expectations, pros and cons, and potential risks. If needed, find a mentor to discuss your plans before taking the leap. I've done this multiple times throughout my career, and it's made all the difference.

Just be sure the person you're learning from shares values that resonate with your own, both in business and in life. A mentor can offer guidance, perspective, and experience, but it's crucial to remember that their path isn't yours to replicate.

Instead, approach mentorship as a conversation. Stay open, ask questions, and take only what serves you. The rest, you'll shape for yourself. That's how I've approached my own growth, and interestingly, over time, I've found myself stepping into the role of mentor for others on the creative journey. It's one of the most meaningful shifts I've experienced, and I consider it a profound honor.

When life presents challenges, whether in self-development or business growth, decisive change is often necessary. The truth is, things won't always flow seamlessly. During those moments when I feel stuck, I ask myself:

"What is at the root of my unhappiness right now? What needs to change? Because this isn't working for me anymore."

The answer always varies depending on the root cause, and could include hiring help, renting more space, or stripping things back to basics. These are tough choices, and the path forward isn't always obvious. Gaining clarity requires patience and mindfulness.

**Knowing Myself:**

Whatever the size of our operations, as our projects and our business grow, they also become more complex, and maintaining a creative identity becomes increasingly vital. I've already talked about how, in larger productions, it becomes necessary to keep our concepts manageable and clear enough for crews or collaborators to execute faithfully. But now let's dive into identity and project management beyond logistics. When it comes to artistic autonomy, we begin to ask the big questions, such as what it means for the work itself.

I came of age in the 1990s, and like many from that era, I was profoundly shaped by grunge culture. One pivotal moment that has stuck with me was the untimely death of Kurt Cobain, the lead singer of Nirvana. His meteoric rise and the fame that followed served as a haunting cautionary tale to all creatives about the cost of losing artistic autonomy.

In the aftermath of his death, his wife, Courtney Love, shared a final letter. In it, he expresses feelings of being jaded by the fame and the industry that had consumed him. What he truly wanted, it seemed, was the freedom to create his work on his own terms and share it with his people, his tribe, without compromise and when he wanted.

I understand this is an overly simplified version of a much more complex story. But I want to illustrate how crucial the toll that creative disconnection can take on mental health. Fame, success, viability, and commercial validation are not substitutes for authentic artistic fulfillment. And they are not always aligned with joy. As creatives, we must be vigilant in protecting our sense of purpose. We must ask ourselves what we truly love about the work and then hold fast to that, even when the world outside pulls us in other directions. It requires courage to push back against commercial paradigms and prioritize what makes us feel alive.

**Holding Strong:**

Of course, what gives me the ability to prioritize this kind of creative integrity, this slower, more intuitive pace, is also tied directly to my personal circumstances. It's important to acknowledge that I don't have children. I mention this because it directly impacts how I structure my time and finances. I know many others, especially those with families and mortgages, may not have the same flexibility. That said, this isn't meant to be a determining factor for anyone starting their own creative business. This is my story, and it holds its own validity. The reality is that the number of floral professionals raising children far outweighs those who are not. Still, I can't separate my decision-making process from my circumstances, just as I can't ignore the struggles my mother faced when she started her own floral shop while raising two teenagers with limited resources.

There have certainly been moments when I should have accelerated growth, but instead slowed down. Most recently, this occurred just before I started writing this book. By spring 2022, the city buzzed again, businesses reopened, kids returned to school, and New York pulsed with life. Everything around me screamed, "Now is the time to scale up!" But I wasn't feeling it. I focused on my fine art practice and portfolio and, for the first time, was okay with that, which would have been unheard of pre-pandemic.

Over the years, I've forged strong friendships with floral professionals at the market, and our discussions reinforced my instincts. We observed the first wave of silent quitting among freelancers. Supply chain issues persisted, while inflation in floral production skyrocketed. Although the news reported a 12% increase in goods, I estimated that floral prices rose closer to 30-40%. With fewer projects, more designers vying for the same clients, and rising costs making everything feel unsustainable, I didn't want to play that game.

I had just spent two years cultivating a process that produced deeply personal art. I realized that ramping up would risk losing the creative momentum I'd fought hard to build. So, this time, I chose myself instead.

To put it simply, not having children was a significant factor in that decision. Without the added pressure of providing for a family, I could afford to commit a few more months to my art. Those were lean months financially, but in terms of personal growth, they were exponential. And I have carried this feeling forward to date. Taking it one day at a time, holding onto that artistic integrity as long as I can.

**Tell Your Unique Story:**

This brings us to our final point, in which I encourage us to use our time and lives as inspiration and motivation for what we create. Life is both valuable and finite. Each of us is given the opportunity, right here and now, to express our unique experiences. That personal truth is the purest source of inspiration we will ever have.

Louise Bourgeois is often quoted as saying, "Tell your own story, and you will be interesting."

I've truly embraced this idea. Despite how painful, traumatic, dull, or even embarrassing our stories may appear, they are uniquely ours and cannot be replicated. Since no one else has had the same life experiences, sharing them through our art is one of the most valuable gifts we can offer back to the world.

That said, let's be honest: it's not always easy. Especially for those of us who lean introverted, or who were raised to stay quiet, blend in, or keep the hard parts to ourselves. And almost ironically, when we do go 'full extrovert,' we risk being told we're too much, or that doesn't seem like you. Sometimes, you can't win for losing.

But as I've discovered, it's that very vulnerability and opting to take the less obvious path by being radically honest that opens something up. And what comes through that break might be your most powerful work.

**Fit and Finish:**

Life is messy at a minimum. And for some of us, it's felt like we've been dragged through every mud pit imaginable. No one is exempt from life's challenges. The difference is that, as artists, we have the ability to transform that chaos into meaning and beauty that resonates.

Florists and creatives alike often navigate uncertain terrain. But it's in those uncertain moments that our commitment to our craft, our values, and ourselves is truly tested.

As we've explored, building a routine that works on schedule is the foundation, allowing our work to thrive. But so does learning when that schedule needs to allow for rest. Creative sanctuaries aren't defined by square footage or aesthetics; even a fold-out table in the corner can be a sacred space. Defending that space isn't selfish. It's an act of self-respect.

Through perseverance and resilience, we develop the tools to navigate this work, often learning from those who have walked before us. Like many of us, I've had to learn to trust my instincts, even when external approval tried to steer me off course. This includes times when I faced doubt or (self-)criticism.

The backbone of it all is the creative process itself.

It's the thing that keeps nudging us forward, even when the path ahead feels like a mountain range made of sand. It's a centered mantra urging us to:

**Surrender. Trust. Keep Going.**

And yes, this work can be demanding, emotionally, physically, and spiritually. Simply making the art isn't enough. We have to care for the mind that makes it, each step along the way.

Learning to lead with patience and humility allows us to see failure for what it is: an opportunity for growth. Hold fast to the small pivots, because in the full arc of a career, those are the choices that change everything. Take the time you need to listen to your heart. Reach out when the path gets too heavy. And start over, when you have to.

Our life's work isn't just made of the polished things we show the world. They're built from the doubt, the grit, the gut-punch failures, the last-minute pivots, and the people who held us up when we couldn't stand on our own.

We don't all start in the same place. That's the truth. Don't ever let anyone make you believe that's a weakness. Measure your progress against your own journey, not anyone else's.

Ultimately, this involves accepting the messy and often ugly aspects, discovering beauty within them, and safeguarding the remarkable mind that creates meaning from it all.

Pace yourself as you move forward. Keep what matters. Let go of what doesn't. Clean up your messes, both within and without. Find the places that YOU fit in. Tell your story. Leave your mark, creative being.

Thank you for reading and taking the time to be here. For choosing to share your light in a world that needs it now more than ever.

Be brave.

Be thoughtful.

Be decisive.

And above all, stay ***Undefined Naturally***!

## Reflections:

– What truly drives your desire for growth or expansion?

– How do you currently define success, and how has that definition evolved?

– Where in your practice is there still room to start fresh?

– How do you protect your creative authority and voice, especially under pressure?

## Tempering:

- What part of your story are you still afraid to share, and what might be waiting for you on the other side of that vulnerability?

- Where does your creative practice find meaning today, and where is it still searching?

- What would you say to your younger self, standing at the starting line?

- How has this book helped you reflect on your own journey and the courage it takes to tell it?

- What truths do you want your future self to remember from this moment?

# PART IV:
## METHOD

From vision, story, and philosophy, we now ground ourselves in hands-on practice, where ideas find their form in the Doing.

# 14

## EVENT PRIMER

In this final chapter, we shift gears and dive into the straightforward, practical work of producing a floral event, start to finish. What follows isn't a comprehensive manual, nor is it specifically for bridal work; there are plenty of those already available in the world. This is more of a walk-through, an offering, where I review the approach I've developed over the years to structuring timelines, developing sample arrangements, presenting them, and conducting client conversations, all of which came about through countless rounds of trial, error, and revision.

Think of this instruction as <u>one working method</u> among many, or as a framework you can lean on and adapt to your needs as warranted. Because I know that, as I started out, I often didn't know where to begin or what should come next, as I fumbled around organizing my time and tasks. So even though the steps are simple, and it remains a true 'primer', they have all been hard-won. And honestly, sometimes that's all we need, something steady enough to direct us where to begin and then send us in a general direction.

# I. Client Request

Peak event seasons (April–June and September–December) see a rise in client inquiries, mainly from organizations I've previously worked with. For annual events, such as nonprofit gala dinners, they often request a fresh take on last year's decor. If I'm still working with the same contact person, I usually have a sense of what to expect. If not, I prefer to make my protocol clear and direct from the outset, so that there is no wasted time or priorities excluded from the beginning.

In my responses, either via email or over the phone, I typically schedule a time to tour the venue and meet with the committee chairpersons. In an ideal scenario, the general timeline would give me about two weeks to present my concept, followed by approximately thirty days until the event date. But let's be honest here; in recent years, timelines have shortened (thanks to the Amazon next-day delivery effect), and a fifteen to twenty-day leeway now feels like a luxurious launching pad. No matter, before making any significant plans, I prefer to wait for an in-person walk-through or, at the very least, a detailed phone conversation. This allows us to delve into the vital aspects of the project together.

One thing I will almost always do is review the organization's website, social media presence, and current branding to ensure alignment. I also ask my contacts to share any inspirational photos, mood boards, or visual decks they might have prepared. For larger corporate events, these visual aids are typically standard practice, as they help multiple teams from various departments stay on the same page while circulating directives internally.

## II. The Budget

A quick but crucial note on budget: it should always be top of mind. With repeat and corporate clients, they are generally straightforward. The floral budget is a line item that is typically set early, often a year in advance. If I've worked with them, I can usually trust their payment procedures. For new clients or tight timelines, I make sure I get a deposit or a signed contract before beginning any work. No exceptions.

Recognizing the ultimate budget limit is crucial, particularly when dealing with larger organizations. This guarantees fair compensation for the services and products I offer. While it may seem obvious, if I hadn't encountered this mistake early in my career, I wouldn't feel the need to highlight it here. I remember several instances when, early on, I fulfilled client requests that exceeded the initial budget, mistakenly believing I could adjust the invoice later, only to discover that those amounts weren't authorized, forcing me to eat the costs, due to their accounting department's limits.

## III. The Walk Through

Full days at my studio during event season are rare. Other than quick stops to grab materials or tools, I'm usually on the run. One of the most common tasks during this time is going on walk-throughs.

If I have an assistant or intern with me, I make sure they understand their role before we head out. While gathering supplies, I hand them a notepad and lay it out clearly:

"Alright, so your job is to take detailed notes: numbers, times, colors, where flowers are needed... everything, basically. No opinions, no interjections unless I ask. If you have something important to mention, whisper it to me. This is not our show, got it?"

They nod. "Got it."

"Good. And above all, LISTEN. These meetings aren't about proving how creative or charming we are. They're about understanding what the client wants. Some of these Committee Heads have donated serious money, and they have strong opinions. Sometimes, they don't even work for the organization; they're just calling the shots because they wrote a check."

At the meeting, I make a point of introducing myself to the key players: the organization's contact, the venue rep, and possibly the caterer.

"Thanks for meeting with us today," I say, shaking hands. "If it's alright, I'd love to start by discussing florals and installations."

During these interactions, I carefully observe both verbal and nonverbal cues to grasp the overall mood. These silent signals are critical and often disclose the following:

1)  Who is ultimately making the decisions?
2)  Are there any underlying tensions within the group dynamic that might be best avoided?
3)  Are silent discrepancies revealed between what's conveyed in emails or texts and what's expressed in person, particularly by the Chairs?

If multiple Chair Heads are present, tensions can rise. Power struggles happen. If things start going sideways, I stay neutral. If the conversation drags unnecessarily, I have a go-to exit strategy:

"This has been so helpful," I say, casually checking my watch. "I do have another meeting in fifteen minutes, so let's make sure we've covered everything floral-related before I have to dash."

During the walk-through, I make sure we get clear answers to all the essential questions:

1)  How many guests are expected?
2)  What's the evening's timeline?
3)  Where's the event entrance? Is check-in digital? Will the table need decor?

4) Is there a cocktail reception? How long is it? Does it need decor?

5) Any pre-dinner entertainment, photo backdrops, or special features?

6) What's the vision? What are you hoping to communicate through the centerpieces? (Sometimes the answer is "nothing," and that's fine.)

7) Is there a changeover? If so, what's the plan?

8) Stage decor? Pipe and drape? Room divisions?

9) Restroom, VIP Lounge, or Green Room decor needed? Think of it this way: If a celebrity entertainer were making a surprise appearance, would she have somewhere fabulous to freshen up?

10) Will guests want to take the flowers home? That affects our pickup logistics.

11) Table shapes? Round or long? Dance floor decor? Suspended pieces?

12) Any special requests from the Chair Heads? Let's talk centerpiece height now before it becomes an issue later.

13) Venue logistics: Trash policy? Water sources? Arrival time? Candle policy? Service entrances? Parking? Storage? Load-in logistics?

Before I leave, I always, **always** walk the load-in route.

"Let's take a walk," I tell my assistant. "I need to see exactly how we're getting everything inside and out for breakdown."

You'd be surprised how complicated it can be, twisting through narrow halls with boxes of flowers, maneuvering past kitchen staff. It's all part of the job, and it's better to know ahead of time.

When the meeting wraps up, I shake hands again. "Thank you all for your time. You can expect the estimate and some images within a week. If we're cutting it close, I'll make sure to get it to you at least a few days before the sample presentation."

For last-minute estimates, I adapt. "I'll send over a shortened timeline ASAP so we can keep things moving." Every meeting is a mix of logistics and human nuance. The clearer we are on both, the smoother the rest of the event runs...And with that, we're off to the next task.

# IV. Estimates

Creating estimates can be challenging and, quite frankly, a real pain. In the beginning, I'd spend hours researching vases, making mood boards, sourcing every detail, only to get ghosted. It was brutal. Eventually, I learned this hard truth: not every inquiry is serious, and not everyone values your time the way you do.

"Are you just comparing prices, or do you feel we're a good fit?" This blunt question helps filter out casual inquiries. If they're only shopping around, I give a general estimate and save detailed proposals for paying clients. I'm not here to hand over a shopping list someone else can copy and undercut.

Most clients don't realize (or don't care) how much effort goes into preparing an estimate. That's why, for particularly intricate proposals, especially those requiring 3D diagrams or unique material sourcing, I charge a fee. This fee rolls into the deposit if they book, ensuring my time is valued either way. This minor tweak alone has saved me countless hours and naturally filters out non-serious inquiries.

So, how do I actually put together numbers? I start by setting a retail budget for each piece, say $X per large urn arrangement, as I am known for this type of work. Then, I divide this by my markup (usually four times the wholesale cost, as many flower schools teach). This gives me my purchasing budget. From there, I figure out what I can buy and whether it's enough to fill the intended vessel.

> *Pro Tip*: *A cost-saving trick I use is incorporating in-season local foliage to bulk up arrangements, reserving delicate (and expensive) flowers like anemones and sweet peas for intimate moments, unless, of course, we're working with a luxury event budget.*

Students often ask, "But what if I don't know how much to order? Can I just use your template?" Sorry to disappoint, but it doesn't work that way. You need to understand your client and the event to develop a pricing method that fits your business. There's no magic formula, just experience, trial and error, and some good old-fashioned legwork.

If I don't have an initial budget to work with, I break things down to their smallest parts. I start with a simple request list, plug in wholesale prices, multiply by my retail markup, and build from there. A simple example using centerpieces, which will more than likely be on the request list, is as follows:

**Example For Fifteen Centerpieces:**

| | | |
|---|---|---|
| 15 | Glass Cylinders x Cost = | Material Cost |
| 5 | Roses x Cost = | Floral Material Cost |
| 3 | Ranunculus x Cost = | Floral Material Cost |
| 3 | Peonies x Cost = | Floral Material Cost |
| 1 | Bunch Filler Flowers x Cost = | Floral Material Cost |
| 1/2 | Bunch Foliage x Cost = | Floral Material Cost |

Now:

- Add + All Floral Material Costs = Total Wholesale Cost
- Multiply the Total Wholesale Cost X by your retail markup (%) = Per Centerpiece Total
- Multiply that Per Centerpiece Total X 15 = Grand Total

*Pro Tip: Know your margins. What do you want to take home after expenses and taxes? My margins hover around 30-33% depending on the season, meaning I make about $0.30 per dollar charged after covering costs. But since I run a service-based business with low overhead, this works for me. If you're starting out, do your research or consult a financial pro. There's too much to cover here, and I don't want to lead you astray.*

Once my estimate is solid, I add in all the extras: trash bags, wire, equipment rentals, labor (about 13-18% of total sales), delivery, breakdown fees, and taxes. Numbers don't lie... but bad math does.

At this stage, I either send the estimate to the customer or, for new clients, specifically, I'll outline my payment schedule needs. A 50% deposit is required to secure the date. No deposit, no work. For short-notice events, I provide a vague initial estimate and send a separate 'Agreement to Begin Work' along with the deposit request. This agreement states that the estimate is subject to change as details are finalized. Since some legal departments and private clients hesitate over non-refundable deposits, I include a clause allowing refunds up to two weeks before installation, but only for the deposit itself, not for any already purchased materials or rendered services.

As for contracts, I strongly recommend working with a legal professional or at least reviewing examples from rental companies (I pieced mine together this way early on). A pro bono lawyer at a NYC small business seminar later helped refine mine. The key takeaway is never to start work without a deposit or a signed contract. Ever.

Once the estimate is approved, the contract is signed, and the deposit is received, we shift gears into execution mode. This includes all the unglamorous but critical back-end planning that makes the event actually happen, like flower counts, ordering, and booking my crew. That's where the real logistics begin.

# V. Mood Boards

---

Mood boards have become one of my most practical tools. They are both for my own organization and to help clients see the vision as well. Still, you might be wondering, 'Do I really need a mood board? Isn't that a little excessive?' Well, if prepping for an event or upcoming project...The answer is yes, you will need one! The thing is, this item will be your visual road map to the forthcoming project and a valuable reference during the entire process. Preparing mood boards is one of those invaluable skills you'll always use as a creative, even if it happens to be an online collage.

When working with large corporate entities, it is becoming normal for 'the Group' you are working with to send you a visual deck of inspirational images, if not a completed mood board. You'll also usually be provided something ready-made if an event planner is on the job.

If not, it will be up to you to create one independently. Aspects which should be included in a mood board for floral events are:

- container/vase options
- candle/lighting options
- linen and chair (cushions)*
- diner setting (tableware) options*
- color story
- flower choices
- floral design inspiration for the arrangements to show the style that will be used
- pipe and drape curtain options*
- misc. Decor items (objects will be used as added interest, like mirrors for centerpieces, for example)
- Including images of the venue for reference, where these elements will be used, is also helpful.

*If you are in charge of the rental items, include these and suggestions for your first choices. <u>ONLY IF</u> they apply to what you are in charge of....don't step on an event planner's feet if they've picked out those items!

**Never underestimate the power of a good mood board**, as it will come in handy as a visual reminder, especially as the complexity of the details begins to mount up. These are great tools to include as additions to your estimate proposals for already committed customers, and for use during the presentation, as providing visuals helps clarify your vision as you sell the dream.

# VI. Calculating Crew Hours

Once a vision for an event is locked in, the next major challenge is assembling the right team. Balancing time, skill, and budget is an art in itself. And that means answering a key question: How many people do I actually need to get this done?

### Key Questions to Ask When Staffing a Project:

1) Will there be large installations?
2) Am I creating branch or urn arrangements?
3) How many centerpieces will be needed?
4) How many cocktail table arrangements are there?
5) Is there a room turnover or timing restriction limiting my access to the space?
6) Is this a 'Union' venue?
7) Will the setup be messy? (Moss, suspended elements, shedding materials.)
8) Are there extensive tabletop elements? (Glassware, vases, candles.)
9) Will any elements be suspended or require ladders?

Each of these factors impacts time, crew size, and overall efficiency. Let's break down this list, starting from the top.

### Breaking Down the Time Estimates:

1) Large Installations &
   2) Monumental Urns

- If mechanics are prepped beforehand, fresh flowers are added on-site.
- A 3'-4' urn arrangement takes ~45-60 minutes per person to make, plus ~20 minutes for cleanup.
- If multiple pieces are required, a two-person team is ideal, but don't expect time to be cut in half; team coordination takes extra time and effort.

    ***Pro Tip:*** *If the team you are working with already knows what they are doing, then we can expect the following, as a rough estimation. For five urns, a team of two finds a rhythm and can finish them faster as they go. So, think 3.5 to 4 hours instead of 5, if there are no major hiccups.*

3) Centerpieces
    - If making 30 centerpieces, each takes 30 minutes: Add 15 minutes per piece for the freelancer's time → 45 min per piece
    - 30 centerpieces x 45 min = 22.5 person-hours
    - If using three freelancers: 22.5 ÷ 3 = 7.5 hours per person (That means if one person did all the work, it would take them 22.5 hours. With three freelancers, divide that by 3 = 7.5 hours per person.)
    - Factor in breaks → This becomes a 9-9.5-hour day for a 3-person team.

    ***Pro Tip:*** *Centerpieces are best done the day before the event unless they need to be built on-site.*

4) Cocktail Tables & Candles
    - Often overlooked, these take longer than expected, especially when you're exhausted!
    - Factor in extra time for lighting candles; it's slower than you think.
    - If setting up 30 tables with 3 pillar candles + 5 votives each, expect: 2 people x 1 hours = 2 labor hours (as a general estimation)

- Add buffer time if the venue is large or spread out.
  ***Pro Tip:*** *If possible, pre-light candles briefly, then blow them out; they'll relight faster on the second lighting.*

5) Room Turnovers & Time Restrictions
   - THIS IS OF THE UTMOST IMPORTANCE!!  Please make sure this is addressed in the walk-through or initial discussions.
   - Late access to a space = 30% more crew needed.
   - Clients don't always understand why rush setups cost more; educate them!

6) Union Venues
   - Know the venue's rules ahead of time; some may restrict tools, ladders, dollies, and what you are allowed to carry in or move.
   - Union house rules are always set up in their favor, NOT yours.
   - You're on the Union staff's schedule, not yours; **<u>plan extra time!</u>**

7) Messy Setups
   - If working with moss, berries, flocked branches, etc., consider hiring extra "clean-up helpers."
   - Messy setups slow down production significantly.

8) Glassware
   - Handling glass is labor-intensive; transportation, setup, and final cleaning all take time.
     ***Pro Tip:*** *Even when pre-cleaned, clear glass always needs a final polish before hitting tables.*

9) Suspended Elements & Ladders
   - Ladder work takes exponentially longer, safety first!
   - Plan more crew time for tasks that require ladder work, scaffolding, or work involving heights.

**<u>Lessons Learned: Planning for the Unexpected</u>**

- Installations will always take longer and cost more than expected. Add time buffers and funds to your plan.
- Overstaffing can be inefficient and costly. Too many freelancers can lead to people standing around, unsure of what to do.
- Mindful planning of labor is an investment. It prevents stress, keeps the budget in check, and leads to smoother execution.
- Remember this harsh truth: From the freelancer's perspective, they are there to put in billable hours, so if something takes longer than you expected, that becomes a 'you-mismanagement' problem.

I've worked on high-profile teams with huge budgets where freelancers were waiting, wandering, or diddling around to avoid being sent home early. That's wasted money. So, please take the time to calculate how much help you actually need and know who you are working with, within and without.

# VII. The Mock-Up Samples

Over time, I developed a production process that helped me create more innovative floral arrangements for large-scale events. I also found that documenting the process properly is just as important. It took some trial and error, but I grew to love the process.

Mock-ups, in particular, have now become one of my favorite parts of the job. There's a kind of play in it as I mix and match containers, candles, and flowers until a clear story begins to emerge. From there, I pare the possibilities down to just two or three strong options. In this mock-up stage, we also address practical questions that arise regarding availability, pricing, and, most importantly, whether the choices truly align with the event's overall vision.

**<u>Key Considerations When Creating Mock-Ups:</u>**

1) Balancing Cost & Options
   - I create three versions: one that slightly exceeds the budget, one that stays on budget, and one that's more budget-friendly.
   - Each version includes notes on materials, costs, and time required.

2) Ensure Quality Across All Options
   - Even the most budget-conscious sample should feel substantial and well-designed.
   - Occasionally, I'll include a stripped-back version just to show what the budget <u>really buys</u>.

3) Estimate Labor with Timing
   - I loosely time myself to estimate labor.
   - I always factor in the difference between real build time and design trial-and-error time.

4) Document the Process
   - I take photos and videos of raw materials, assembly (especially mechanics), and final arrangements.
   - This prevents reverse-engineering headaches later on. (Been there: chin in hand, staring at a photo like, how the hell did I build that?)

5) Refine the Sales Pitch
   - While building, I mentally rehearse how I'll present it.
   - By the time we do the tasting sample, I know the piece inside and out and can pivot based on feedback.
   - We're selling the complete vision, not just some flowers.

**Managing Client Expectations:**

During this stage, clients often ask for photos of what I'll be presenting. I DO NOT send mock-up photos until the official tasting presentation. Why? Because prematurely sending photos can invite a flood of opinions, suggestions, and unnecessary revisions, all before the design is even finalized.

Instead, I send images of individual elements I plan on using (vases, flowers, candles, etc.) and let them know: "It's our policy not to share unfinished inspiration until it's ready for presentation."

If they insist, I don't lose the gig over it. If pressured, I ensure the visuals are well-lit, curated, and aligned with the look I want them to remember.

**Final Thoughts:**

Mock-ups are a critical step in visualizing the final product, as well as for pricing, logistics, and client buy-in. The more polished and well-thought-out the samples are, the more intentional the presentation will feel, and the more confidence your clients will have in the final result. Set expectations early, but keep the presentation polished no matter what.

# VIII. Visualization

Visualization is common in elite sports, but I rarely hear florists or artists talk about it, and that's a shame because it's one of the most useful tools I use. The concept is similar to manifestation techniques, but here, I'm talking about a much more practical application, one I use nearly every day. Bear in mind that this differs from the Observation we explored in the chapter on the Creative Process.

For me, it's about mentally rehearsing a process before it happens. Like when I used to run track, I'd walk through hurdles in my mind before hitting the starting line. In business, this means mentally walking through my day, whether it's planning for an event, or rehearsing a meeting or presentation. When I have a floral sample presentation coming up, my mental checklist often looks like this:

*I walk into my studio early in the morning and turn on the lights. The flowers look good except for one or two that didn't make it. I swap them out. I remove my blazer and dress shoes and change into comfortable work shoes. I put on my apron and check the cooler for extra flowers. Remember to bring extra flowers. I pack the arrangements carefully, checking the stems so they don't bruise. The boxes feel light. Do they need more water? I'll bring the small watering can and paper towels for any spills. I text the driver to confirm pickup time. Tools are in my bag, wait, I need to add trash bags...*

And just like that, I've built a mental to-do list before even stepping into the studio:

**<u>Mental Checklist:</u>**
1) Pack extra flowers
2) Bring a watering can
3) Grab paper towels
4) Confirm the driver's pickup time
5) Add trash bags to the tool bag

This mental rehearsal prevents forgotten details and helps me anticipate potential issues before they arise. It's an invaluable skill that takes practice but becomes second nature over time.

That said, I also believe in going into meetings with an open mind, like a blank canvas. Yes, I'm there to present my work, but more importantly, I'm there to listen.

The worst thing you can do in a creative meeting is take feedback personally. If a client isn't vibing with something, ask questions: What specifically isn't working for them? More often than not, the issue is easily fixable, a small adjustment rather than a total overhaul.

# IX. The Presentation

Like visualization, presentation hinges on preparation. When I go into a meeting, I do so, having already mentally rehearsed it, but also with the understanding that things may shift as the conversation unfolds. The best way to present yourself and your work is to remain adaptable, stay calm, and be confident in your value.

A significant aspect of self-respect is how we present ourselves, both in our demeanor and in the quality of our work. This goes far beyond dressing sharp or speaking confidently. It's about sharing our understanding of our value and helping others see it too.

**Before the Meeting:**

When it comes to presentations, preparation is everything. On the day of, I like to arrive at my studio early, ensuring my samples are flawless before packing them up. I never bring more than two or three options. Too many choices can overwhelm a client. I also triple-check that I have all the small but crucial details: lighters for candles, mood boards, sample fabrics (if relevant), and, of course, my trusty tool bag. A dossier with estimates and mood boards is also essential for quick reference.

Once I arrive at the venue (always early), I set up quickly, making sure my first arrangement is ready with the appropriate fabric swatches. Over time, I learned to always start with my favorite. I'm not sure when I adopted this habit, but I've noticed it leaves a strong initial impression. Some real estate agents use a similar approach, leading with a stunning property first to gauge a client's interest before moving to more practical options. In events where time is money and not everyone stays for the entire meeting, making that first moment count is powerful.

**Presenting With Confidence:**

During the presentation, I avoid jumping straight into pricing details. Instead, I focus on selling the vision, the dream of what the event could look like. Money talk can sometimes make people uncomfortable, so I let the organization's staff or decision-makers handle the specifics. That said, I'm always ready with numbers if they come up. I never fumble when discussing my pricing; I own it.

If a client asks about costs, I pivot smoothly:

"Yes, this option is slightly higher, by X% or $X, but let me show you what you're getting."

**Confidence is everything.**

Throughout the meeting, I kept my energy up and my enthusiasm high. I answer questions but don't linger too long on any single arrangement. I also make sure to document everything. A quick snapshot of each setup is invaluable, especially when last-minute changes come up later. With multiple events in a season, memory alone isn't enough; photos ensure I deliver exactly what was promised.

When presenting, I start with the premium design, move to the mid-range, and end with the most budget-conscious option. If there's hesitation or pushback, I don't take it personally. Over the years, I've trained myself to see these moments objectively, as if I were presenting on behalf of <u>someone else I deeply respect</u>. It shifts my mindset from defensive to problem-solving. Clients aren't always great at articulating their concerns, so it's up to me to decode their reactions.

**Reading the Room & Handling Feedback:**

For instance, one time, a client recoiled at an arrangement and blurted out:

"What is this? This looks dead!"

Not exactly what you want to hear. But after some conversation, I realized the yellow flowers and variegated foliage reminded her of old lilies and autumn decay. The fix was simple: no yellow flowers, no variegated leaves. Crisis averted; though I've had a lingering distrust of yellow flowers, worried others equate yellow with death, ever since.

Transparency is another key element of the presentation. If I'm working with a tricky floral season, I'll acknowledge it upfront:

"These fire-orange tulips should be available, but recent storms in Europe have caused delays. If necessary, we'll substitute with a similar variety to maintain the aesthetic."

Clients appreciate honesty, and setting realistic expectations builds trust.

Toward the end of the meeting, I transition into larger-scale arrangements and installations, walking clients through vessel selections and floral choices. If I'm dealing with an especially intricate installation, a 3D rendering can be a game-changer for helping clients visualize the final product. And no, you don't need to outsource this; there are plenty of affordable, even free, user-friendly design tools available online.

Once all questions are addressed, I wrap things up by confirming that I'll send finalized estimates soon. This subtly signals that the deposit process should already be in motion. As I discreetly pack up, I make a point to thank everyone for their time before making my exit.

I've done dozens of these, but it still takes something out of me every time. So I always end with the same ritual: a deep breath, a bold exhale, and a coffee.

# X. Flower Counts and Ordering

Once the estimate is locked down and finalized, I begin compiling my flower order. This is where the process involves a lot of counting and some extrapolation: pulling the items and numbers I've already included in the estimate and then breaking them down into specific counts for each arrangement.

**Ordering Checklist:**

<u>Pull Numbers from the Estimate.</u>

- Break down each arrangement into specific stem counts: roses, filler, foliage, etc.

<u>Create Recipes by Arrangement Type.</u>

- If you have multiple centerpiece styles, make a recipe for each and total everything.

<u>Account for Hard Goods.</u>

- Vases, materials for mechanics, rentals, and <u>order these early</u> in case of delays.

<u>Coordinate with Your Wholesaler.</u>

- Share your delivery and installation schedule. Let them guide product timing.

<u>Plan for Substitutions.</u>

- Have backups ready, and don't alarm the client over minor changes....because they will happen!

<u>Estimate Labor & Crew Needs.</u>

- Use your flower count to update project staffing and collect W-9s.

**I usually end up with individual lists for all these items:**

- One Master List with ALL totals, items, areas with flowers, vases/containers, etc.; basically, the detailed and expanded estimate with total costs and numbers to keep track of every flower and dollar in real time.
- One list covers everything (but without the dollar amounts): Event sections, flowers assigned to each arrangement, and their placement (lounge, cocktails, centerpieces, main floor, etc.). That list also serves as the recipe sheet for freelancers, outlining their pre-production responsibilities.

- One list of ONLY total flower counts to share with my wholesalers for ordering.

   *Pro Tip: If you have multiple vendors, create separate individual lists to make it easy for them. Make duplicates for yourself and include a header with the vendor used, your name, and EASY-to-read contact information, and a date/time you need the arrangements at your door, and make that note. Some florist use the date of their event instead, and that will have your flowers arriving late, so fair warning!*

- The same rule applies to all hard goods orders (e.g., vases, urns, tape, floral foam, buckets, etc.), which must be sent out first.
- Lastly, I have a list of vendors, crew, and delivery personnel with their scheduled dates and times, which helps me keep track of billable hours. Having their contact information on this list is also very helpful.

You'll get faster in this whole process with practice, but even then, it's never perfect. So remember to be kind to yourself.

Lastly, as you plan for your crew, use this moment to adjust your staffing needs and collect W-9s (and subcontractor contracts, if applicable) from freelancers. This saves you from end-of-year paperwork nightmares. Being organized now is a gift to your future self.

*Rule of Thumb: Yes, there will be hiccups. Sometimes the peonies don't come in. Sometimes the lisianthus arrives limp. This is normal. Don't freak out. Your calm professionalism will keep confidence intact even if you're pivoting last-minute behind the scenes.*

# XI. Initial Prep Work and Floral Arrivals

Successful installation work requires a balance of instinct and focused attention. This begins to truly come together in the way you handle preparations as materials arrive. I always start with hard goods, because it's a quick win that clears mental space and keeps everything moving smoothly as the time-sensitive materials arrive closer to the day of the event. I place orders for any hard goods ASAP if I'm not buying directly from my wholesalers in the flower market. Once the hard goods arrive at the studio, I open all the boxes and physically check each item.

> **Pro Tip:** *Please avoid the mistake I made early on, assuming all was well because the boxes weren't rattling. Also, just because a bill of lading states that X number of items are included doesn't mean they are all there. Humans still pack many things, and humans miscount all the time! This applies to any direct-shipped flowers as well.*

Likewise, believe it or not, sticker and label removal can be a full-time job. I've lost entire afternoons peeling stickers from the bottoms and sides of glass vases. Ask any floral designer, and they'll tell you it's the bane of event prep. Ideally, I complete all of this at least ten days before the event. This buffer allows time to reorder any broken items and ensures that the week leading up to the event is all about flowers.

For most flowers, three days before arrangement-making is ideal. However, some flowers, such as roses, lilies, and amaryllis, require more time. Certain rose varieties take six to seven days to peak in a cooler. Lilies and amaryllis vary depending on your climate, ambient temperatures, and other factors. My best advice for true beginners? Contact your wholesalers and ask them when they recommend receiving the product for peak freshness.

I'm a firm believer in properly conditioning flowers whenever possible. Yes, it's extra work, but the product holds up better and lasts longer. One way many people 'market' flowers for big events, myself included at times, is by simply cutting the bottoms and placing the bound and wrapped bunches directly in water. This works if you're short-staffed or using the product immediately.

However, the preferred method is individually cleaning each flower, cutting them roughly to size, and letting them sit at least overnight in a cooler or cold room. This hardens them off and gives them a good drink before use. I also like adding a visible label with the flower count on each bucket to track how many flowers are in each one.

Regardless of your method, please ensure the flowers drink, and if possible, DO NOT use them right out of the box. Even to this day, I've gotten cocky, rushed the process, and invariably been burned.

*Side Bar: This is all I'll say on the matter of flower-specific care because there is far too much to cover in this basic primer. Additionally, there are tons of resources available on the individual treatment of flowers. I recommend researching best floral practices, speaking to your wholesalers, and allowing yourself a bit of grace as you build your floristry skills and knowledge.*

Before the full production day, everything should be laid out so freelancers can get straight to work when they arrive. This means having a completed floral sample made and ready, a detailed and clear recipe with flower counts, and an objectives list for the day ready to go.

# XII. Day of Event Production, In-House

Every event prep day starts with a short crew meeting to align on expectations and timing. This section focuses on the in-house production days, typically at our studio, a rented auxiliary workspace, or the event location, where materials are pre-transported.

On in-studio prep days, while the team focuses on centerpieces, I turn my attention to any last-minute mechanics that need refining for large installations or on-site arrangements. Early in the day, I check the flowers to make sure we have everything we need and replace anything that isn't holding up. I also touch base with the client to confirm that nothing has changed, no last-minute additions, no sudden subtractions.

Next, I pull and label flowers for pieces that will be created on-site. This is also a great time to get a head start on medium-sized arrangements, like bar pieces or small floor gardens that are manageable to transport. If garlands are needed, I prefer to make them in advance. In the afternoon, once the centerpiece production is in a good place, I pull a team member to assist with any remaining pressing projects.

When it comes to transportation, balancing pre-assembled pieces with on-site work is key. Finished arrangements take up far more space in the van than raw materials, so planning ahead is essential. Large urn-style pieces, for example, are almost always completed on-site due to their bulk and delicate nature. The decision of what gets built in advance versus what is created on-site ultimately depends on available transport space, time, and crew size. Having a solid, actionable plan prevents last-minute scrambling and ensures a smooth, stress-free event execution.

**Recap Checklist:**

<u>Morning</u>
- Crew briefing
- Flower quality check
- Client touchpoint

<u>Midday</u>
- Pull and label on-site materials
- Mid-size arrangement prep

<u>Afternoon</u>
- Garlands, short-lived floral applications, or things that will go 'out of water' assembly
- Load-in prep

<u>End-of-day</u>
- Confirm the transport plan
- Pack up as much as possible

A smooth prep day means I leave the studio tired, but not anxious. That's always the goal.

# XIII. Packing Up and the Tool Bag

As arrangements are completed, I have the crew start packing them unless they need to be stored in the cooler overnight. If an arrangement does require refrigeration, I place it in the cooler without a box. The humidity inside a cooler will make cardboard boxes soggy overnight, leaving them weak and unstable. However, I always prep the boxes and packaging in advance so we can quickly transfer the arrangements into them the next morning.

**Packing:**

Packing centerpieces is one of the rare instances where I still use cellophane, especially for shallow containers like compotes. Water will inevitably slosh during transport, and if it spills, it can weaken the cardboard, leading to catastrophic collapses, something I've unfortunately witnessed firsthand when boxes gave out just steps from a venue door. To be more sustainable, you can use contractor trash bags, which at least serve a second purpose, or opt for a heavier-weight plastic drop cloth that can be cut to size and reused multiple times.

Metro Racks, wire shelving units on wheels, are a game-changer for pre-packing and organizing transportation. Anything that can be packed in advance is stored on my Metro Racks overnight, making for a seamless loadout the next day. These racks are also perfect for Sprinter vans. My go-to size is 18 inches deep, 4 feet long, and 5 feet tall, the ideal dimensions for maneuvering through New York City's tight hallways and elevators.

Wrap any remaining urns, vases, or pedestals now.

*Important: If you custom-painted any vessels, don't store them in a cooler or wrap them with paper before they are fully cured. Moisture will wreck the finish, and paper will stick to tacky paint (ask me how I know...)*

**Prepping Gear:**

Finally, I gather any specialized tools we might need for the job. And yes, I always have a list for that, usually one I start compiling days ahead of time, adding to it as the event approaches. That said, I also maintain a standard, pre-filled, event-ready tool bag stocked with all the essentials. This tool bag is never used for day-to-day studio work; it's reserved exclusively for on-site event production. While it's an extra investment, it makes the entire operation significantly more efficient.

**<u>Here's what's always inside my Event Tool Bag:</u>**
- A wide variety of florist waterproof and standard tapes
- Extra floral knives and Clippers
- Wire cutters
- Spool wires and a couple of different gauge wires
- Microfiber towels and a full first-aid kit
- Sharpies
- Lighters
- T-pins
- Box cutter
- Staple gun (JT21) and florist stapler
- Glue gun
- Measuring tape
- Water tubes in various sizes
- Flower food packets
- Gloves and zip ties
- Misting bottle
- Small dust broom

This level of preparation ensures that, no matter what challenges arise, we're always ready to handle them efficiently.

# XIV. Loadouts and Deliveries

Getting materials where they need to go, on time and intact, requires a reliable system and trusted subcontractors. Without help, delivery and breakdown would be impossible, especially in a city like Manhattan, where efficiency is everything. That's why hiring professional delivery crews has become one of the most cost-effective and practical solutions for my business.

Always, always remember that flowers are the heart of our work, the very thing the client is paying for, so protecting them during transport is non-negotiable. There's no sense in spending a week meticulously caring for each bloom only to mishandle them during load-in and load-out. This is where hiring professional delivery crews is worth every penny; their expertise ensures that arrangements arrive intact, looking just as stunning as when they left the studio.

One of the biggest hurdles in event logistics is accurately visualizing how much will fit into a transport vehicle. A fully loaded van can look very different from what you imagined when designing the event. To help with this, I'll break down what typically fits into a standard Sprinter van.

First, be aware that Sprinter vans come in different lengths, so always check ahead if you're renting or considering a purchase. Regardless of size, how much you can fit depends heavily on how well you pack and your use of rollable metro racks.

**Sprinter Van Packing Overview:**

**<u>Rack Capacity Example:</u>**
Each rolling Metro Rack (my go-to: 18"D x 48"W x 60"H) can typically hold:

- 4 low rose boxes per rack
- 3–5 standard centerpieces per box, depending on size
- 2 racks = 24–40 arrangements
- My regular driver keeps one rack in his van at all times

→ **Max capacity across three racks: ~36 standard arrangements**

*Pro Tip: The top box must be removed before rolling into the van (interior height is approx. 6 feet). Once inside, boxes can be restacked.*

### Extra Space Accommodations:

After the racks are loaded, a long Sprinter van can also fit:

- 2 stepladders (tucked under racks)
- 4 large urns
- 3–4 rose boxes with tall arrangements
- Bundles of flowers in water buckets
- Low tubs or dishes with pre-built floor gardens
- Tool bag + small boxes (e.g., votives or candles)

*Pro Tip: Secure racks to the van walls using zip ties or bungee cords to prevent tipping in transit.*

### Pricing, Delivery, and Breakdown Services:

If you're a new event florist, you're probably wondering, How much should I charge for delivery and breakdown? The short answer: do the math. Although we thoroughly discussed breaking down costs into clear, quantifiable elements in the estimates section, it is also worthwhile to share another example of applying this method to delivery service fees. Presenting it as a line item can help clients understand why the costs are adding up.

1) Van Rental Cost: How much does it cost to rent or lease a van for the day? Remember, the U-Haul $19.99 deal on the sides of vans is never the actual bottom line cost!

2) Labor Cost: How many people do you need to load and transport the arrangements?

3) Hourly Rates: What is the pay rate for your delivery crew?

4) Time Estimate: How long will loading, transporting, and unloading take?

5) Breakdown Crew: How many people will you need to return, break down the event, and transport materials back to your studio? Spoiler: It's almost the exact same cost as the initial delivery.

6) Additional Costs: Gas, tolls, and parking fees all add up; don't forget to include them in your pricing.

Once you calculate these numbers, apply your pay rate accordingly. If hiring independent contractors, **be realistic and upfront about how much product you're moving.** The delivery and breakdown service I use is expensive, but they are among the best in the industry, so I pass the direct cost to the client and add my 12% markup to cover overhead and insurance.

Yes, independent contractors are required to carry their own insurance, but I maintain my own coverage as well to ensure full protection. These details matter for financial clarity and maintaining professional operations.

# XV. Installation Day Of Production

On-site production is central to how I run my studio, especially here in Manhattan. In fact, it's one of the main reasons I've been able to keep my team small. But pulling off a seamless day-of installation depends heavily on the venue, and that's why I always discuss logistics during the initial walk-through.

For most galas, cocktail hour starts around 6 or 7 p.m.; luncheons usually begin around 11 a.m. Either way, I arrive as early as possible. Often, the pace of setup is dictated by catering, specifically when tables are "popped" (set up) and linens are "dropped." Until then, there's usually not much you can do.

**How Many People Do You Need?**

Let's say your installation includes pre-made centerpieces (approximating around 20 arrangements), a couple of urns, and a small pipe and drape section. This said, I'd probably bring:

1 freelance floral designer

1 person for pipe and drape

1 general helper

**But please stay realistic with yourself and your crew's skill level.**

The designer gives you breathing room in case of delays or last-minute changes. The helper and tech support keep everything flowing, and visually, it looks more polished to have designated roles. But if you're just starting out and the budget only allows for you and one assistant, that's completely fine, too. Don't sweat it; just make sure to leave yourself more time to complete the job.

**Arriving & Loading In:**

First thing: check in with venue contacts to confirm staging areas and load-in access. I might ask for a couple of spare tables, but always confirm ahead. Remember, space is often tight.

Even if I've worked at a venue before, I still check the layout again. <u>Don't assume anything.</u> Once you're staged, tackle the largest, most complex installs first, like urns, archways, or drapes. Do these while your energy is high and your hands are still clean.

> **Pro Tip:** *Build large pieces as close to final placement as possible. Saves time, reduces lifting, and prevents water spills or damaged finishes. If using cachepots or painted vessels, fill them while they're still wrapped, and don't remove the wrapping until they're in place.*

**Setting Tables & Votives:**

Once the big installs are done, move to centerpieces. If they've been stored in a cooler overnight, they may "sweat" from condensation. Bring microfiber towels to dry them off before placing them.

Now is also the time to set out votives and leave them ready to be lit as close to the start time of the event as possible. If catering is lighting them, hand off a few long-tip lighters; 3 or 4 is ideal for around 200 votives. It's a small thing, but it earns goodwill fast...and gets you home earlier.

> *Pro Tip:* Cluster allocated votive sets together on each table with wicks up. Light them right before guests arrive. For 40 tables with eight votives each, this saves the dizzying merry-go-round dance and a lot of time.

**Clean-Up & Documentation:**

Before you pack up, clean your workspace. If the venue has storage, use it. If not, either reload your boxes or coordinate a return pickup, especially if you'll need those same boxes for breakdown.

At this point, you can usually send your team home. But before you leave, document the room!

I deeply value the work of professional photographers. Their eye and artistry bring an entirely different dimension to an event's documentation. My own photos are never meant to replace those, only to ensure I have timely and practical images for my portfolio and marketing needs.

Early on, I relied solely on event photographers for images of my work, often signing long usage contracts and then waiting months for a handful of shots, few of which were useful for my personal marketing. That experience taught me to always bring a DSLR and photograph my own installations.

> ***Photo Tip:*** *Take more than you think you'll need. Different angles, different lighting, different exposure settings. It'll take time to sort and edit later, but one killer image is worth the effort.*

Phones work well for behind-the-scenes clips, but nothing compares to a proper camera for crisp, detailed images, especially in low-light conditions.

And if your budget allows, bring in a photographer yourself. It not only elevates your portfolio but also invests back into the craft, with artists helping artists.

# XVI. Breakdown and Wrapping Up

The event may be over, but the job isn't done until the breakdown is complete, and the return of tools and materials to your studio is handled with care. This phase is just as important as setup, especially if you want to protect your gear, reduce waste, and maintain your sanity.

If you've got composting protocols, use them. If not, it's worth considering. Even small steps, like separating out green waste, can make a meaningful difference over time.

A game-changer for me has been training my delivery team to return everything organized. I can't tell you how demoralizing it is to walk into the studio the next day and find it piled high with trash bags and unlabeled mystery boxes that rattle with the sound of broken glass.

With a well-trained crew, this doesn't happen. They arrive for breakdown with labeled containers, a plan, and enough help to get the job done efficiently. I happily pay for an extra hour of their time to ensure everything is sorted and returned properly. What would take me hours, they complete in one, with care and order.

**Donation & Inventory:**

If flowers or plants are being donated, I separate and prep them immediately for redelivery. The rest of the vessels, risers, candles, and hardware, I pack into clearly labeled storage boxes.

**Each box gets:**

- Event Name
- Date
- Contents
- Quantity

This system makes tracking inventory easy, and helps me see what's actually being used. At year's end, I review and donate what hasn't moved to organizations like Materials for the Arts. My rule: **If I haven't used it in a year, it's out.** Space is expensive in NYC. Streamlining is self-care.

**Reset & Review:**

Before I mentally "close the box" on an event, I always check my event tool bag. What needs to be replaced? Anything missing or broken? These small resets in between jobs make a big difference when you're heading into the next one.

I also carve out a quick 10–15 minutes for a personal debrief:

1) What worked really well?
2) What missed the mark?
3) How accurate were my counts for flowers, materials, crew time, and delivery hours?
4) How did the team function?
5) Were there timing issues?
6) Did the crew size match the workload?

This reflection draws clarity at the end of a long project. It's a simple, ego-free check-in that helps me prep smarter next time.

If you're managing back-to-back events, this kind of review isn't optional; it keeps you sharp and on the right track.

**Mark the Moment:**

Last but not least: celebrate.

Seriously.

You just executed a full-scale event, and that is no small feat. Maybe it's a quiet night in, an ice cream stop on the way home, or a proper dinner out. Whatever it is, mark it. You did something big.

That moment of reflection and joy matters just as much as the perfect centerpiece.

# ACKNOWLEDGEMENT

Some things come together in silence. Some are shaped by sheer presence.

This book made it here because some people knew when to say exactly what was needed and when to say nothing at all.

For all the friends, family, clients, and supporting hands who have contributed, to those who have purchased the work over the years, and to all those who may never read these words:
Your gestures, both large and small, have helped in ways that words could never fully express.

***Thank you.*** You know who you are.

# ABOUT THE AUTHOR

Juan M. Villanueva is a second-generation florist-turned-multidisciplinary artist and entrepreneur based in Manhattan. After leaving art school, he spent over two decades building a practice rooted in persistence, intuition, and everyday beauty, bridging private floral events, site-specific installations, painting, and bioart, drawing on more than thirty years of immersion in the floral world. His hands-on approach has led to artist residencies, solo exhibitions, and international teaching engagements alongside the steady rhythm of commissioned projects.

In "*Undefined Naturally,*" his first book, Villanueva distills a lifetime of experience into a raw meditation on creativity as both a service and a means of finding balance. Blending essays, personal field notes, and a 16-point floral event primer, he offers practical wisdom and emotional clarity for florists, artists, and anyone navigating the inner work of making a living in art.

# VISUAL HISTORY

What follows is a short visual history, fragments of a life in process. These images span decades of creative work, family memory, and quiet labor: teaching, painting, building, living. They are echoes of the work that shaped the words.

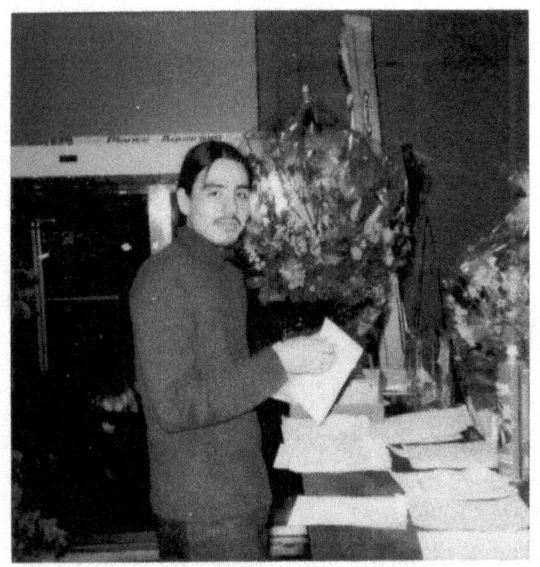

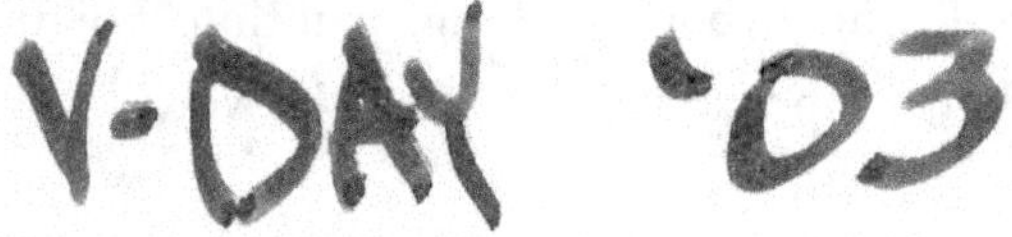


**Valentine's Rush**
Chicago
c. 2003

In the final days at the flower shop before my move to New York City. Valentine's Day orders stacked high, double-checked with care. Captured by the shop owner.

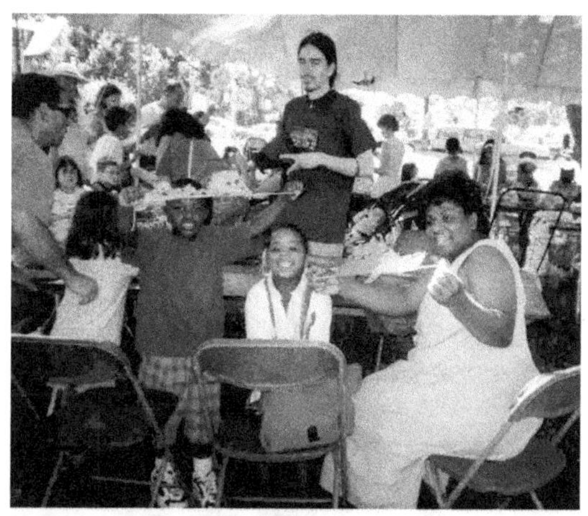

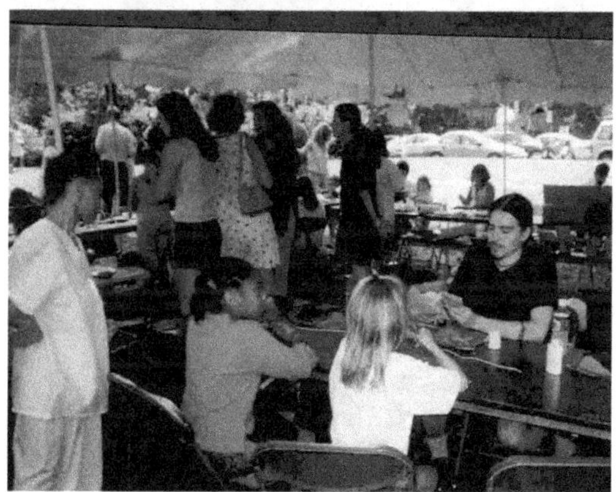

**Evanston Ethnic Arts Fair**
**Teaching 'Papel Picado'**
c. 2000

Sharing the vibrant tradition of papel picado through a hands-on workshop that brought joy to both children and adults. Rooted in my Tejano heritage, this moment reflects a continuing legacy of cultural celebration, expression, and the power of communal making. Captured by the event's press team.

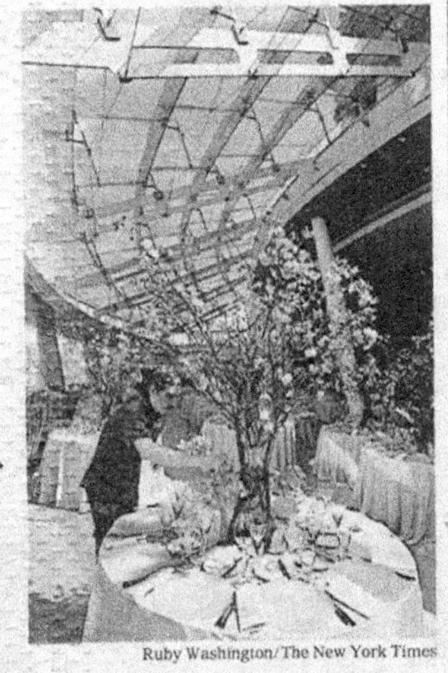

Ruby Washington/The New York Times

**A Grand Gesture in Brooklyn**

The Brooklyn Museum prepares to open its new entrance pavilion tomorrow. An assessment by Herbert Muschamp.  WEEKEND, PAGE E31

**Cherry Blossom Celebration**
New York Times Feature
c. 2004

Beneath a soaring cherry blossom arrangement created for the Brooklyn Museum of Art's reopening, captured during my time at a flower shop on Manhattan's Upper West Side. This image, featured on the cover of The New York Times, represents a moment where craftsmanship met cultural celebration. Photo by Ruby Washington / The New York Times, 2004.

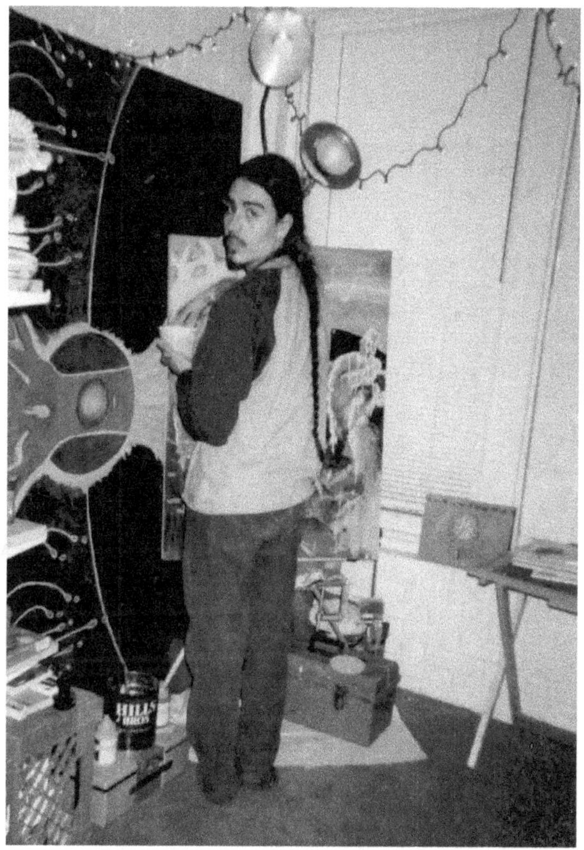

**Sunroom Studio, Working in Oils**
Chicago
c. 2000

A private moment in my home studio, where long hours of experimentation and reflection took shape on canvas. My long, braided hair draped down my back as I worked, absorbed in the process. Captured candidly by my wife.

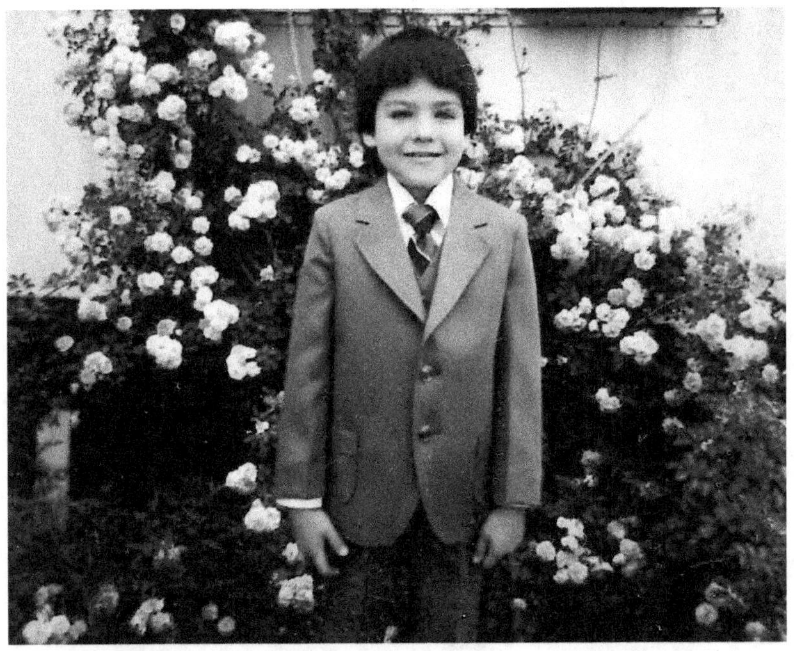

**Pride and Roses at the Ranch**
South Texas
c. early 1980s

Here I am in front of my grandmother's personally prized climbing garden roses. Probably dressed up for first communion, no one could quite remember. Photo by mom.

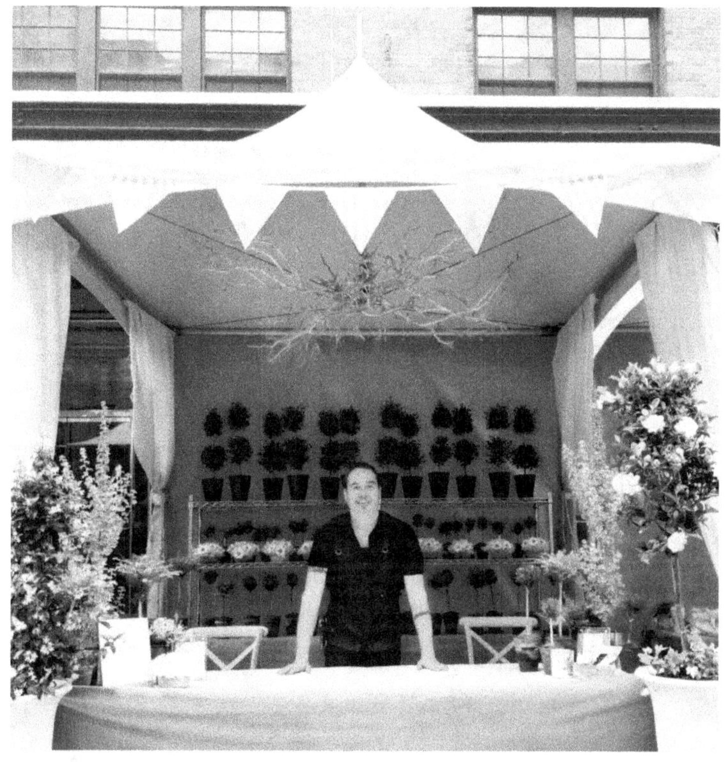

**Festival Topiary Booth**
New York City
c. 2021

Working my topiary booth for a city-sponsored floral festival,
following the pandemic closures. Photo by G. Kosciuk.

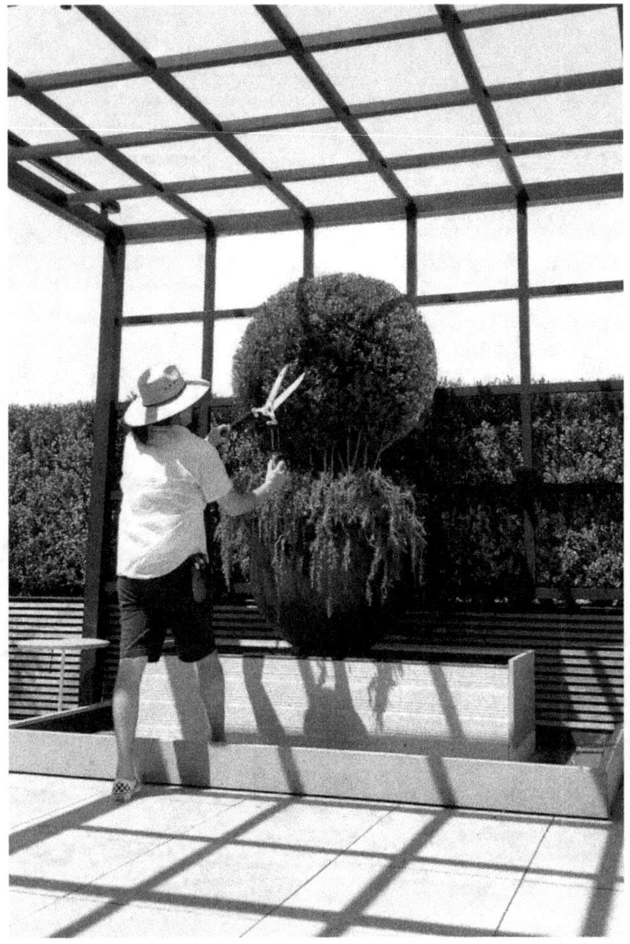

**Essential Services Topiary Artist**
Manhattan
c. 2020

Perched in a fountain, I add finishing touches to one of the topiaries in a private client garden as part of my gardening practice during the COVID-19 lockdowns. Speaks to the power of a diverse work portfolio, scale, and labor in motion. Video still by me.

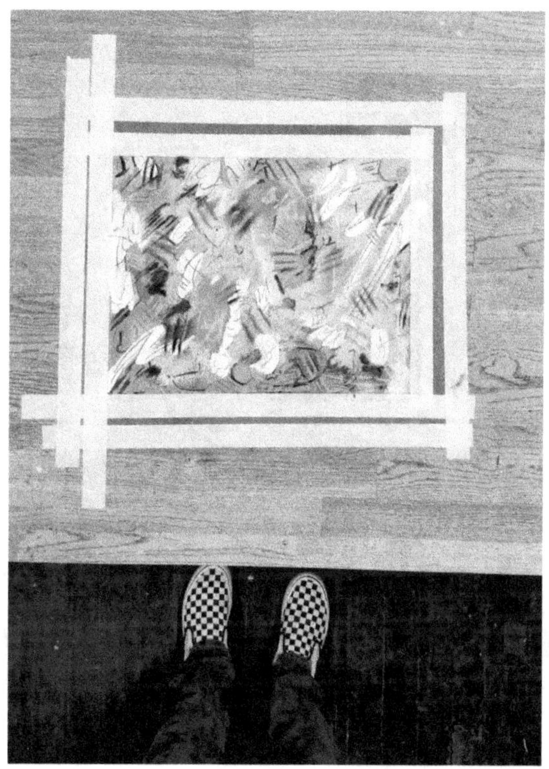

**'From the Workbench'**
Manhattan
c. 2018

The catalyst for my eventual art revival came after years of stepping away to build my floral design company. It was a tongue-in-cheek version of making art as a Florist, but little did I know that this little piece would stir up a longing that I didn't know I held onto. Photo by me.

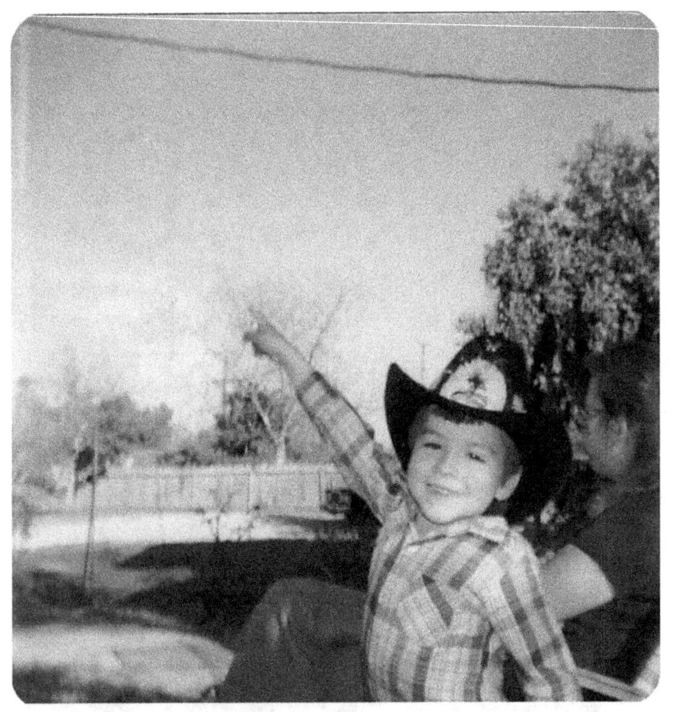

**Childhood Moment**
South Texas
c. early 1980s

Me around 6 or 7 years old, donning a cowboy hat and shirt, pointing up to the sky, a gesture of curiosity and wonder. My mother lounges beside me, watching with quiet presence. Always looking up and outward, just as I have been throughout life.

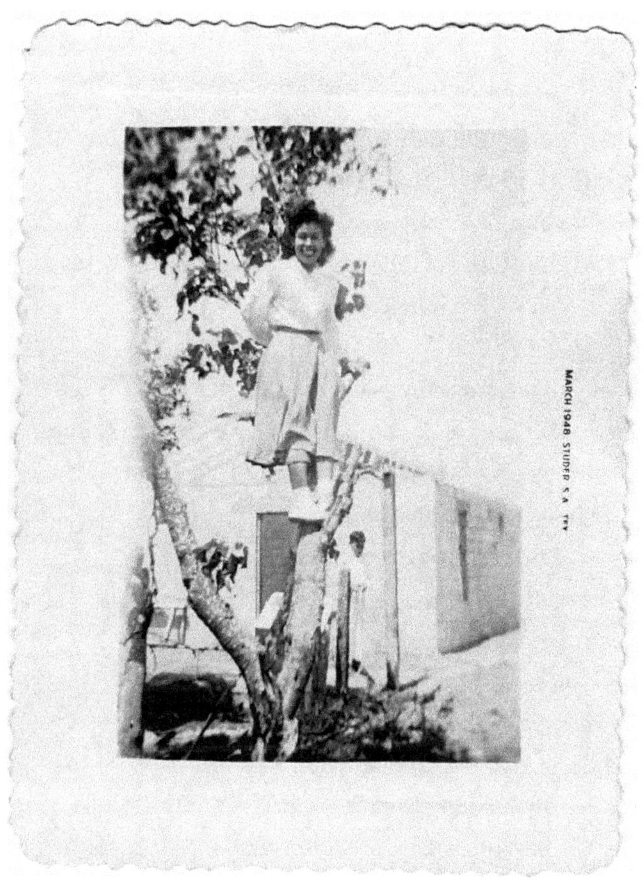



**Our Matriarch**
South Texas
c. 1948

*Abuela*, my grandmother, around 21 years old, stands proudly perched in a tree she climbed, wearing a poodle skirt and bobby socks. A gentle defiance and spirited playfulness shine through, a wild, untamed Tejana spirit she has carried her whole life (celebrating a 99th birthday in 2025), and one that lives on in the generations that have followed.

# Appendix A: Continued Reading

Here's a curated list of works, not a formal bibliography, but a short collection that has stayed with me in the studio and the making of this work. Some are instructional, contemplative, or personal, each leaving an indelible mark.

- *The Artist's Way* — Julia Cameron
- *A Collaboration with Nature* — Andy Goldsworthy
- *Abstraction In Art and Nature* — Nathan Cabot Hale
- *Women Who Run With the Wolves* — Clarissa Pinkola Estés
- *The Power of Now* — Eckhart Tolle
- *Tao Te Ching* — Lao Tzu
- *In My Family / En mi familia* — Carmen Lomas Garza
- *Family Pictures / Cuadros de familia* — Carmen Lomas Garza
- *Santa Barraza: Artist of the Borderlands* — Santa Barraza
- *Ancient Texas* — A. Joachim McGraw
- *Curandero* — Antonio Noé Zavaleta, Ph.D.
- *The Four Agreements* — Don Miguel Ruiz
- *The Alchemist* — Paulo Coelho
- *Arranging Flowers* — Shozo Sato
- *Picasso: A Portrait* — Gertrude Stein
- *Think and Grow Rich* — Napoleon Hill
- "The Practice of Shipping Creative Work" — Seth Godin, interviewed by Chris Williamson, *Modern Wisdom Podcast*, 5 Nov. 2020, YouTube.
- "Lessons on Creativity with Rick Rubin" — Rick Rubin, interviewed by Jay Shetty, *Glo*, 26 Aug. 2024, YouTube.

# Appendix B: AI-Assisted Editing and Refinement Disclosure

This memoir is a personal account rooted in lived experience, written and developed by the author. While the narrative remains entirely original, artificial intelligence (AI) tools were used to support aspects of editing, refinement, and structural development. Specifically, AI-assisted processes were employed to:

- Improve grammatical accuracy and stylistic clarity
- Offer alternative phrasings to enhance readability
- Provide organizational and structural suggestions

All AI-generated recommendations were selectively considered and further adapted by the author to preserve the authenticity, voice, and intent of the work. The manuscript was also reviewed using plagiarism detection tools (such as Grammarly) to ensure originality and prevent inadvertent inclusion of external material.

No AI tool was used to research, generate, or supply factual content. All research, lived experience, and source material originate solely from the author.

AI assistance was used strictly as an editorial aid. No content was included without thorough review and modification to ensure alignment with ethical and legal standards, thereby ensuring that the final text reflects the author's lived experience and creative vision.

AI tools referenced include OpenAI ChatGPT (GPT-3.5 and GPT-4) and Grammarly, accessed between 2022 and 2025. This disclosure is provided in the interest of transparency and to acknowledge the evolving nature of authorship and editorial tools in contemporary creative practice.